HOW WEATHER WORKS

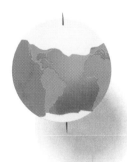

HOW WEATHER WORKS

ROB DEMILLO

Illustrated by
PAMELA DRURY WATTENMAKER

Ziff-Davis Press
Emeryville, California

Development Editors	Melinda Levine and Kim Haglund
Copy Editor	Kelly Green
Technical Reviewer	Dave Clark
Illustrator	Pamela Drury Wattenmaker
Project Coordinator	Ami Knox
Proofreaders	Ami Knox and Carol Burbo
Cover Illustration	Pamela Drury Wattenmaker
Cover Design	Regan Honda
Book Design	Carrie English
Graphics Editor	Dan Brodnitz
Word Processing	Howard Blechman
Page Layout	M. D. Barrera
Indexer	Carol Burbo

Ziff-Davis Press books are produced on a Macintosh computer system with the following applications: FrameMaker®, Microsoft® Word, QuarkXPress®, Adobe Illustrator®, Adobe Photoshop®, Adobe Streamline™, MacLink®*Plus*, Aldus® FreeHand™, Collage Plus™.

If you have comments or questions or would like to receive a free catalog, call or write:
Ziff-Davis Press
5903 Christie Avenue
Emeryville, CA 94608
1-800-688-0448

ISBN 1-56276-228-1

Manufactured in the United States of America
✪ This book is printed on paper that contains 50% total recycled fiber of which 20% is de-inked postconsumer fiber.
10 9 8 7 6 5 4 3 2 1

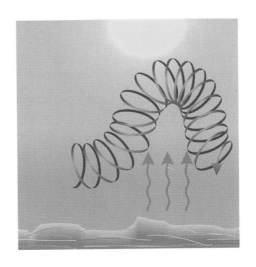

To dearest Kate.
Without her encouragement,
I would have torn up the
author's agreement a long time
ago...

And to my four-legged pal Max,
who gave up six months of
weekend walks in the woods...

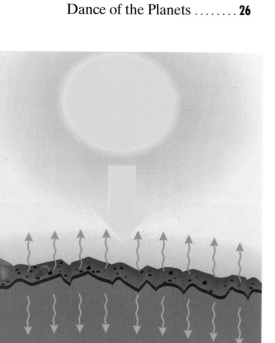

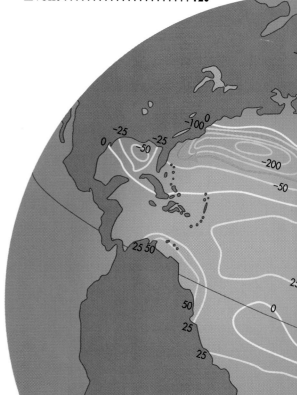

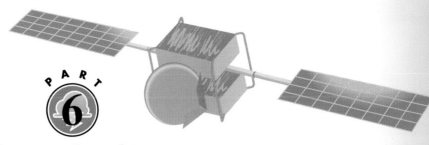

PART 5

Microclimates and Unusual Natural Phenomena
130

PART 6

The Atmosphere of Our Neighbors
152

PART 7

Human Activity and the Atmosphere
168

PART 8

Etcetera
208

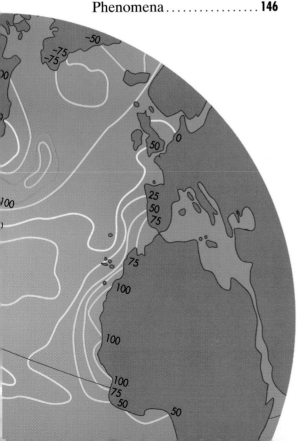

Although it's been said before, it's nonetheless true: No book is the work of a single person. The number of people to thank are far too numerous, so I'll just touch on a few: my mother and father for encouraging the best in their kids; the high school teachers and college professors who didn't just read their topics from a textbook, but presented them to me with a sense of wonder; the people at Lincoln Laboratory's Weather Sensing Group for giving more detail to my own, personal internal weather model, and to the untold thousands (millions?) of weather professionals and enthusiasts on the Internet that helped me compile some of my more recent information.

Specifically, I would like to thank Dave Clark for his amazing technical prowess. (Without Dave, you'd be reading about several real interesting weather "facts" right now.) Thanks to Pamela Drury Wattenmaker for transforming my stick-figure sketches into the beautiful graphics you see on these pages. Thanks also go to the folks at the University of Michigan's Weather Underground Project on the Internet for the myriad images that were used in this book. Jeff Masters is the "cyber-curator" over there.

weath·er —n. 1. The state of the atmosphere at a given time and place, with respect to variables such as temperature, moisture, wind velocity, and barometric pressure. 2. Adverse or destructive atmospheric conditions such as high winds and heavy rain.

—American Heritage Dictionary, 3rd ed.

Before retiring for the evening, a marketing analyst in Chicago turns on the local news to examine the weather conditions in the area for the morning commute. After being informed of an impending cold front that will move down from Canada during the night, she makes a mental note to have the car winterized, turns off the television, and goes to bed.

Despite the modern conveniences of meteorological forecasting and instant access to those forecasts, this scene has been repeated for centuries in one form or another. Sailors routinely checked the condition of the sea and sky prior to undergoing a long journey so they could prepare their ship and crew adequately. Native Americans predicted early winters by observing the trees and the wildlife and made appropriate adjustments in their yearly schedules to compensate. By checking the latest forecasting tools at our disposal, humans have been able to prepare for seasonal changes or day-to-day fluctuations. No matter that these forecasting tools are occasionally wrong; their track record has been proven to be pretty reliable, so we continue to put our faith in them.

Weather is arguably the single most powerful force on the face of the earth. The earth's weather machine was in place long before humanity was present: The power of the wind, water, and sun has been shaping mountains, carving rivers, and eroding continents for billions of years. It is little wonder that people throughout the ages have invested so much time in understanding and learning to cope with the planet's weather. It is an integral part of all of our lives, and our very existence depends on our ability to learn its cyclic patterns and make sense of the portents of inclement weather.

Occasionally, the atmosphere of planet Earth generates events that seem to defy all that we know about the way weather works: a never-ending rain causes a river to overflow its banks by many miles; tornadoes drop out of a thunderstorm, devastating everything in their path, and hurricanes appear out of nowhere to batter hundreds of miles of a seacoast. Earth's weather seems not to be content with these short-lived disasters. Historical records contain evidence of longer-lasting ones such as bone-chilling summers and winters without any snow.

In this era of satellite coverage, up-to-the-minute forecasts, and high-speed computer models, we are surprised when Mother Nature pulls a rabbit out of her hat. We are only now beginning to realize that the weather and climate of planet Earth is not composed of isolated, easily understandable events. Looking at the entire global picture rather than localized events reveals a complex interplay of solar energy, planetary rotation, air-ocean interaction, atmospheric composition, physical and chemical interactions, and the influence of life. In modern parlance, the earth's weather machine is a *chaotic system*, or a system formed by the breakdown of ordered systems with understandable components into a disordered system that exhibits unpredictable events.

In other words, we may be able to understand the parts, but it may not be possible to completely comprehend the sum of those parts. Only now, during the last few years of the twentieth century is modern society beginning to realize what ancient societies knew all along: Weather is a force that we may never fully understand, and as such, it deserves our respect.

If modern society has an advantage over the ancient civilizations, it is that our understanding of the universe is based on scientific principles, not myths and anthropomorphisms of natural events. Science examines the world through a series of models that are based on a set of known physical principles. These models should corroborate each other, as they are all attempting to describe different aspects of the same physical universe. Ideally, the advantage of science over myth and theology is that it is *self-correcting:* If a model does not fit established facts, or if new facts are uncovered to dispute the model, it is thrown out in favor of a new model.

This book attempts to describe what we know, or more accurately, what we *think* we know about the mechanics of the earth's weather machine. The models, and even the facts portrayed in this work should be constantly called into question by the reader. This text should be thought of as a stepping stone to the next level of your interest in the weather; it should not be thought of as the end of the journey. If you learn anything from this book, it should be a sense of inquiry into the natural world of which you are a part.

Rob DeMillo
demillo@ll.mit.edu

A BLANKET OF AIR

CONTENTS

BY EXAMINING EARTH'S size, content, and energy output, astronomers tell us that its parent star, the Sun, is nearly halfway through its 11-billion year lifetime. This seems to be verified by current geologic estimates, which place the age of the Earth at slightly less than half of that figure, somewhere in the neighborhood of 4.6 billion years. Current theories of planetary evolution suggest that the planets of our solar system and our Sun formed from the same interstellar cloud of gas and debris. This theory of formation is called planetary accretion.

It is believed that the current atmosphere's constituent components were trapped in the dust and debris of the original accreting disk and made up approximately 0.01% of the mass of the material. These gases remained trapped in the rock until the planetary bombardment lessened and the planets began their own internal thermal reaction. This internal heat freed the trapped gas in a process known as outgassing.

Today, billions of years later, the end result of this process is an earth wrapped in an envelope of atmosphere scarcely more than 50 miles thick. This thin shell of gas is only about 0.6% of the diameter of the earth, yet it is enough to harbor the only ecosystem in the universe—of which we are aware—and keep it safe from harm. Inside this cocoon of warmth lies not only the protection, but the turbulence and power of the atmosphere that we have come to recognize as our own.

Although we almost never think of it in such terms, the gases that compose the atmosphere have substance and weight like any other matter. As such, it stands to reason that atmosphere has mass, momentum, and dynamics. In a very real sense, we all live at the bottom of an ocean of air. Eddies and currents swirl about our bodies, moving the trees and carving the mountains. Birds cut through our air in much the same way that fish swim through the sea. As any child who has let go of a circus balloon can tell you, floating to the surface of our atmospheric ocean is a simple matter of becoming more buoyant than the gases that surround us.

Science requires that we label the atmospheric strata and classify the clouds, and that is what the first part of this book will do. However, along the way to the cold dissection of the atmosphere, the reader will be taken on a journey which began billions of years in the past, long before our solar system existed. At its end is Now, a time in which intelligent creatures can theorize about their beginnings while looking up to see the clouds dance lazily across the sky.

There is room in science for both fact and wonder.

CHAPTER 1

Earth's Atmosphere— A Life Protrait

ABOUT 5 BILLION years ago, an aggregate collection of dust and gas collected together via a common center of gravity. Eventually, internal gravitation pulled all of the heavier elements toward the center of the dust and gas cloud. The resulting knot of material was the seed that eventually became a living sun, but early on, this center of gravity provided a place for all objects in the cloud to "fall," thus beginning orbital rotation. It was this rotation that eventually gave the cloud a shape: a disk, out of which the planets of our solar system would later form. This theory of planetary formation is known as the accretion model.

The accretion model explains the rough, rocky material of the early planets, including the earth, but does it also account for the atmosphere? Several theories for atmosphere formation have been brought forward since the general acceptance of the planetary accretion model of early solar system formation. These theories range from the primitive planets sweeping up the leftover gas from the original nebula (much in the same way that they swept up the leftover debris), to the constituent gases of the atmosphere hitching a ride on meteors and comets that were constantly raining down on the planetoid.

The theory that has gained the most acceptance, however, claims that the atmosphere never arrived on the new planets, but rather developed from materials that were here all along. These raw materials for the constituent atmospheric gases were trapped in the early planetary formations, either in pockets in the original material, or combined as more complex substances such as calcium carbonates. When planetary bombardments ceased and the new planet's internal heat began to build up, these gases were released. Most of the atoms and molecules were too heavy to escape the local planetary gravitation attraction and, therefore, stayed around and formed the atmosphere. Many of the lighter gases, such as hydrogen, were able to escape into space.

At this point, the terrestrial planets' size, composition, and distance from the sun directed the course of atmospheric composition. Mercury, having a smaller gravity field and suffering from extreme external heating by its proximity to the sun, lost most of its primordial atmosphere and remains a near vacuum today. Venus retained most of its carbon dioxide, or CO_2, in its atmosphere, while Earth's liquid water and calcium content reabsorbed a large percentage of the CO_2 molecule, creating calcium carbonate. The primordial atmosphere of Mars is still a hotly contested issue. Liquid water apparently did flow on the surface at some point in its past, but today, water resides largely in permafrost buried deep within the soil of the planet.

We now see a very different Earth deep in our primordial past than we see today: a newly formed planet with an atmosphere consisting mainly of nitrogen and carbon dioxide, with some water vapor, carbon monoxide, and a small amount of hydrogen. Within the primitive oceans of ancient Earth, a primordial soup of organic chemicals was beginning to stir. The addition of atmospheric lightning began the formation of amino acids, essential building blocks of carbon-based life. Oxygen, the volatile gas required for most life as we know it, did not exist in a free state in the atmosphere of the planet until as recently as 2 billion years ago.

The science of determining atmospheric content in our ancient atmosphere using direct fossil evidence is known as paleoclimatology. Examination of uranium oxide discovered in sediment dating back 2.5 billion years gives students of the early atmosphere the first direct evidence that their atmospheric models are correct: Very little free oxygen existed during that time. Had free oxygen existed, it would have combined with the uranium oxide and formed UO_3. The examination of iron-rich rock beds suggests that about 1.8 billion years ago, free oxygen was suddenly quite abundant. Where did it come from?

Oxygen likes to attach itself to other atoms and molecules to form new molecules. When energy is added, hydrogen and oxygen create water, and abundant calcium combines quite readily with oxygen. The energy from the original formation of the planets still makes itself known in the form of geologic activity and radioactive decay. These processes existed very soon after the original formation of the planet and were mostly responsible for the outgassing, or the release of trapped gases, of various elements from the surrounding rocks. Once the chemistry of the planet had been cooking for a few billion years, oxygen, which was originally released and then retrapped in oceans and calcium-heavy rocks, began to be released again as the heat broke down the chemical bonds holding oxygen to other elements.

Eventually, the released oxygen traveled up to the top layers of the atmosphere, where it encountered intense ultraviolet radiation from the sun. This process produced the molecule O_3, or ozone. A blanket of the ozone molecule is opaque to ultraviolet radiation, so the action of ultraviolet radiation on the atmosphere actually creates a shield through which the life-threatening ultraviolet radiation is unable to pass.

Approximately 450 million years ago, the buildup of ozone was enough to create a window of opportunity that allowed land-based life to grab a foothold.

This was the final key to the permanent establishment of oxygen in our atmosphere: Life itself generates oxygen via photosynthesis of plants. The production of oxygen was now self-sustaining, and the supply became richer as time went on and the earth's biomass exponentially increased. Oxygen was created via photosynthesis, and absorbed back into the oceans and rocks. Carbon dioxide was absorbed by plant life and the oceans and released again through volcanic outgassing. The earth had begun a cyclical progression of absorption, use, and release that continues to the present day.

Planetary Formation and Earth's Oxygen Content

6 On the early terrestrial planets (Mercury, Venus, Earth, and Mars), the gases that were first released consisted mainly of water vapor, carbon dioxide, carbon monoxide, nitrogen, oxygen, and hydrogen. Due to the nature of the rocky material on the surface, however, oxygen was reincorporated into the surface, leaving little or no free oxygen in the atmospheres. A large percentage of the hydrogen, the lightest element, was able to slip quietly away from each of the terrestrial planets' weak gravity fields.

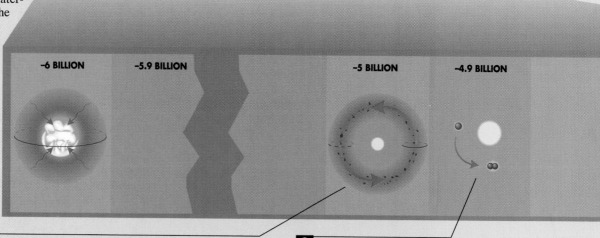

−6 BILLION   −5 BILLION   −4 BILLION

−6 BILLION   −5.9 BILLION   −5 BILLION   −4.9 BILLION

1 As the amount of material in the center of the cloud increased, internal heating built up due to a process called gravitational contraction. Matter continued to rain down on the center of the cloud, and eventually the internal density of the material was such that thermonuclear ignition took place.

2 This ignition stripped away the lighter gases close to the center of the cloud, and left the heavier, rocky elements orbiting about the center: a kind of orbiting rock garden. Eventually, these small rocky particles began to collect together in small knots via the same mechanism that created the infant, or proto, sun: gravitational attraction. In the early solar system, when a small particle's orbit brought it near a larger particle, it fell into the larger object's sphere of influence. If these objects merged via collision, their gravitational fields combined, thereby attracting other nearby objects. This process is called accretion.

3 It is believed that the early phase of planetary formation happened very quickly—about 10 centuries—after solar ignition. During this period, small-scale solid planetesimals, or small planetary bodies less than 5 kilometers in diameter, were formed. Afterwards, the process of building larger planets out of the planetesimals took a great deal more time, on the order of 50 to 100 million years. This stage of the growth process was slower due to a balancing of the ratio between planetoids whose sizes were increased by collision and planetoids whose sizes were decreased by collisions.

7 The energy from the original formation of the planets still makes itself known today in the form of geologic activity and radioactive decay. These processes existed very soon after the original formation of the planet and were mostly responsible for the outgassing of various elements from the surrounding rocks. Once the earth began to heat itself internally, oxygen that was originally released and then retrapped in oceans and calcium-heavy rocks was once again released.

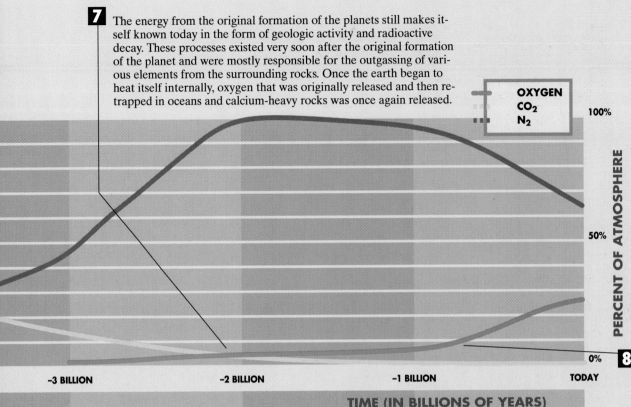

OXYGEN
CO$_2$
N$_2$

100%

50%

0%

PERCENT OF ATMOSPHERE

-3 BILLION   -2 BILLION   -1 BILLION   TODAY

TIME (IN BILLIONS OF YEARS)

8 Oxygen was created via photosynthesis, and absorbed back into the oceans and rocks. Carbon dioxide was absorbed via plant life and the oceans and released again through volcanic outgassing. The earth had begun a cyclic progression of absorption, use, and release that would continue to the present day.

-4.7 BILLION   -4.6 BILLION

EARTH'S CORE

5 The theory that has gained the most acceptance claims that the constituent gases making up the atmospheres were incorporated into the new planets when they were formed. Gas was trapped in the original accreting material, and remained there due to compression from gravitation forces and meteoric impact. Once the impacts stopped, however, the internal heat of the new planet took over, forcing the gas out to the surface in a process known as outgassing.

4 Once these planetoids reached an appropriate size, about 1,000 kilometers in diameter, a final stage of development took place: slow collection of smaller particles by the newly formed larger planetoids. In essence, the new planetoids swept up the remainder of the debris left over from the early, nebulous solar system as these smaller particles fell into the planetoids' spheres of influence. This process possibly took on the order of 100 million years.

The Earth's Atmosphere—Present Day

It is the compressibility of gas that allows dense, moist conditions to exist close to the surface. The overwhelming majority of the mass of our atmosphere lies within about 19 miles of the surface of the earth. The atmosphere above this level becomes rarefied and scarce. At roughly the 50-mile mark, the atmosphere is so thin that weather as we know it is virtually nonexistent. However, even at that height the thin atmosphere is enough to scatter incoming cosmic radiation in all directions.

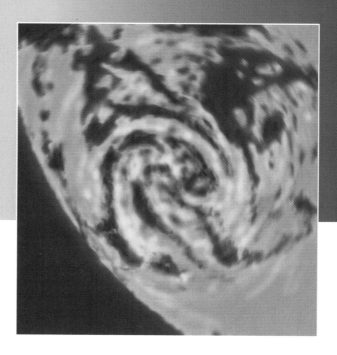

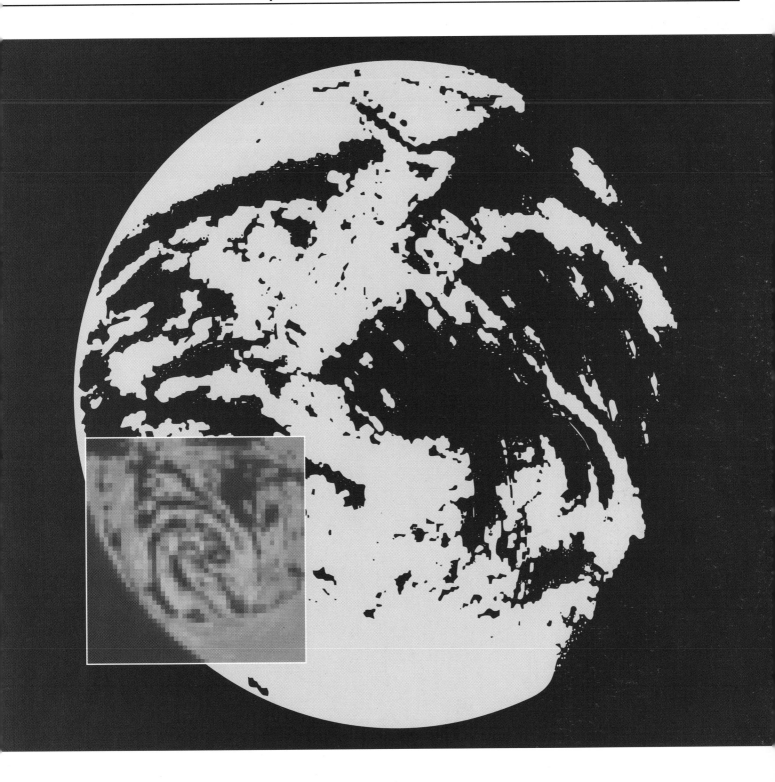

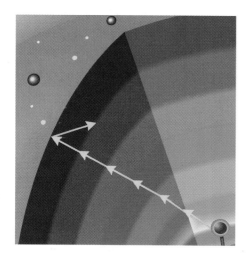

Through the Depths

THE COLLECTION OF gas around our planet is like an ocean. Down here in the depths at which most of the life on Earth exists is where the air is dense and moist. Here, life has the greatest degree of protection from cosmic radiation, debris, and particles from the sun. Having been immersed in this ocean our whole lives, we are scarcely aware that the air above our heads has depth or a surface. And we are certainly unaware that all of this atmosphere looming over us has weight.

At sea level, the tower of air molecules extending some 250 miles straight up weighs down on us with a pressure of 14.7 pounds per square inch. This standard air pressure is used as a unit of measurement, conveniently referred to as 1 atmosphere. Consider that it takes nearly the entire depth of our atmosphere to give us this pressure; although the equivalent weight in liquid mercury would form a 1-inch-by-1-inch column merely 29.92 inches in height, and the equivalent weight in liquid water would form a column only 33 feet deep.

Under normal pressure and temperature conditions, solid and liquid matter are incompressible because the molecules making up the matter are either locked in a lattice or held together by intermolecular forces. Gas, on the other hand, is very compressible since the gas molecules are not bound together and expand to occupy any available volume. Reduce the volume, and the density of the gas will increase. For this reason, the weight of the gas making up the atmosphere compresses itself so that the majority of the mass of the atmosphere stays down near the surface. As a matter of fact, nearly 99% of the mass of Earth's atmosphere lies within 20 miles of sea level.

If we begin an imaginary journey from the surface of the earth straight up through our blanket of air, we notice that air density is not the only factor that contributes to differences in our atmosphere at different depths: Atmospheric temperatures vary remarkably. The first two layers of the atmosphere are called the *troposphere* and the *tropopause*; together they average about 16 miles in depth.

During this first 16 or so miles of the atmosphere, the temperature slowly decreases over a 100° F, from a global average at the surface of about 60° F down to about –70° F when you hit the top of the tropopause. Past the tropopause are two layers referred to as the *stratosphere* and the *stratopause*. Throughout the stratosphere, very little changes in temperature until we encounter the infamous layer of O_3, or ozone.

Ozone is an ionized form of oxygen that is nearly opaque to ultraviolet radiation from the sun. When the ultraviolet portion of the solar spectrum encounters the ozone layer, it is either scattered or absorbed by the gas. This intake in energy causes the ozone layer to warm up slightly, reradiating the energy as heat. This output of heat from the ozone layer causes the atmosphere above it to warm up dramatically. This ozone-related warming causes the temperature of the stratopause to increase gradually until it reaches the temperature of the freezing point of water.

The next two paired layers are the *mesosphere* and the *mesopause*, which together rise to an altitude of nearly 50 miles. Sufficiently high above the warming effects of the ozone layer, the temperature in the mesosphere and the mesopause drops precipitately. As one progresses up through these two layers, the temperature drops to nearly –100° F and the air becomes too rarefied to support life. Many meteorologists consider this altitude to be the top of Earth's active weather atmosphere.

Although the meterologic atmosphere may stop here, the physical blanket of air does not. If our journey continues outward, we encounter the thickest layer of the atmosphere yet: the *thermosphere*, which is nearly 120 miles in depth. Strangely enough, near the top of the thermosphere, a temperature warming trend begins again. Although not as large a temperature change as the stratopause, the effect is measurable. This temperature increase is due to the absorption of incoming radiation by the air molecules in this layer.

At about 170 miles above the surface of the planet we encounter what is believed to be the final layer of atmosphere: the *ionosphere*. The ionosphere gets its name from the condition of the constituent gases of which it is made up. At this height, the atmospheric gas gets a larger dose of incoming radiation than do the layers below. As a result of this radiation absorption, the gas molecules of the atmosphere have become *ionized*, or stripped of one or more electrons.

Finally, just to complete the picture, some mention should be made of the first line of defense that Earth has against incoming solar and extrasolar radiation. Earth's *magnetosphere* is a large magnetic field produced by the planet and it extends out some 40,000 miles beyond the ionosphere. The magnetosphere emanates from the poles of Earth, and as it captures incoming radiation and solar particles, it routes them down to either pole. As the solar particles enter our physical atmosphere, the gas they encounter becomes ionized. The end result is a beautiful aurora display visible in the high latitudes of both hemispheres.

Through the Depths

The nonuniformity of the atmosphere makes its presence known in distinct strata, similar to the layers of rock that one might see in the face of a cliff. The classification of these various strata allows meteorologists to identify certain atmospheric events with their altitudes, providing a better understanding of the way our weather systems operate.

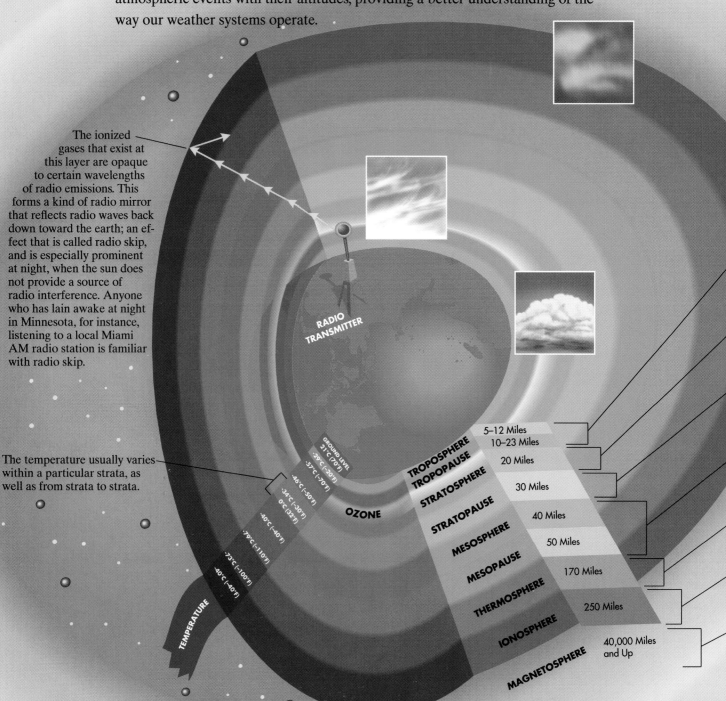

The ionized gases that exist at this layer are opaque to certain wavelengths of radio emissions. This forms a kind of radio mirror that reflects radio waves back down toward the earth; an effect that is called radio skip, and is especially prominent at night, when the sun does not provide a source of radio interference. Anyone who has lain awake at night in Minnesota, for instance, listening to a local Miami AM radio station is familiar with radio skip.

The temperature usually varies within a particular strata, as well as from strata to strata.

RADIO TRANSMITTER

GROUND LEVEL
21°C (70°F)
-29°C (-20°F)
-46°C (-70°F)
-34°C (-30°F)
0°C (32°F)
-40°C (-40°F)
-79°C (-110°F)
-73°C (-100°F)
-40°C (-40°F)

TEMPERATURE

OZONE

TROPOSPHERE   5–12 Miles
TROPOPAUSE   10–23 Miles
STRATOSPHERE   20 Miles
STRATOPAUSE   30 Miles
MESOSPHERE   40 Miles
MESOPAUSE   50 Miles
THERMOSPHERE   170 Miles
IONOSPHERE   250 Miles
MAGNETOSPHERE   40,000 Miles and Up

The troposphere runs from sea level up to about 5 miles at the poles and 12 miles near the equator. The next atmospheric layer, the tropopause, adds another 5 to 11 miles in thickness. It is in these two layers, totaling an average of 16 miles in depth, that the majority of the significant weather in our atmosphere occurs, aircrafts maneuver, and mountains reach their zeniths.

The stratosphere runs to almost 20 miles in altitude and maintains a relatively constant temperature of about –70ºF. It is in the stratosphere that there exists a thin 10-mile strip of an allotropic form of oxygen called ozone, or O_3. This relatively thin atmospheric component is largely responsible for the almost total absorption of solar ultraviolet radiation.

The stratopause extends to nearly 30 miles in altitude, and, curiously, increases somewhat markedly in temperature, with the top layer of the stratopause peaking at just above the freezing mark. When ozone, or any substance, absorbs energy—solar ultraviolet radiation in this case—its own internal energy level increases and thereby generates heat. Even in these rarefied conditions, heat rises and warms the stratopause above.

The next two layers of strata, the mesosphere and the mesopause, rise up to nearly 50 miles in altitude and complete what many meteorologists consider to be the top of Earth's weather-active atmosphere. Rising above this layer is a thin, gaseous world where the rarefied air is too thin to support life and too insubstantial to be able to buffet about solid matter.

This next strata of the atmosphere, the thermosphere, begins at about 50 miles in altitude and is about 120 miles in thickness. The scattering and absorption of radiation by the atmospheric molecules in this layer is enough to once again begin a warming process.

The warming process continues on past the thermosphere into what is regarded as the final layer of our blanket of air: the ionosphere. The ionosphere peaks out at about 250 miles in altitude, and consists mainly of molecules and atoms of atmosphere that have become electrically charged, or ionized, because they are the first line of defense against the sun's radiation.

Although it is technically not a part of Earth's atmosphere, the magnetosphere is the region of Earth's magnetic field that extends out to about 40,000 miles. Large packets of solar material released from the sun via solar flares get trapped in Earth's magnetic fields and ping-pong between the north and south poles of the planet. Near the poles of the planet, these vagabonds encounter the ionosphere at about 150 to 250 miles in height. It is this interaction between the sun, the magnetosphere, and the ionosphere that gives earthbound viewers a spectacular light show in the form of the *aurora borealis* (Northern Hemisphere) and *aurora australis* (Southern Hemisphere) as the particles ionize the free air molecules that they encounter.

Cloud Formations

ALTHOUGH THE WATER-LADEN entities we call clouds were known to be the portent of both fair and foul weather for centuries, the concept of a "cloud" as we know and understand it today did not come into being until the 1800s. Prior to that time, clouds were referred to as essences in the sky. It was understood that dark, brooding essences meant bad weather. For the most part, connections between cloud formations and approaching weather were relegated to the ranks of folklore and legend.

In 1803, the scene changed nearly overnight, mostly due to the work of an English weather hobbyist, Luke Howard, a chemist by trade. He spent much of his time observing cloud formations and their relationship to the immediate weather, and his classifications are still in use today with only minor modifications and additions. Howard's cloud classification scheme used Latin designations and organized cloud types into a logical chart based on two groupings, *heaped* and *layered*, and three classifications within these groupings: *cirrus, cumulus,* and *stratus.*

Howard was one of the first to observe that cloud formations have complete life cycles that start with seed growth, build to maturity, and dissipate back to nothingness. During this process, Howard noted that a given cloud in one grouping or classification could change to another. In order to classify these transitional phases, three new groupings were later added by meteorologists: *layered-heap, precipitating,* and *unusual*. Other cloud classifications were derived by combining existing classifications along with altitude information. For example, a *cumulonimbus* cloud is a cumulus cloud with a high, level tower that produces precipitation.

The basic principle behind cloud formation is simple: vertical transport of water through evaporation and lifting. Moisture trapped in the ground or present in lakes, seas, and oceans ascends to the sky, forming a cloud. The local wind patterns then move the water to another location where precipitation occurs. But how does this happen? Although there are several ways in which cloud formation can take place, there are three main processes at work: convection, orographic lifting, and dynamic lifting.

During *convection*, a water source such as moisture-laden ground or a body of water is heated by the sun, and simple evaporation takes place. The warm surface heats the air immediately above it, which causes it to rise, taking the water vapor along with it. The amount of water vapor that air can hold is a function of the air temperature: The higher the temperature, the greater the capacity to hold water.

The temperature in the troposphere and the tropopause quickly decreases as altitude increases. The change in altitude is accompanied by a reduction in the local air pressure, allowing the rising packet of air to expand as it is cooling. This cooling affects the water vapor in the ascending air, causing water droplets to condense out as it expands. A similar effect can be seen on a glass of cold water in a warm, humid room. The water vapor in the air condenses out as water droplets when the vapor comes in contact with the cool glass of water. The water glass appears to sweat. The temperature level at which this condensation occurs is called the dew point, or condensation level.

Orographic lifting is a variation of the convection mechanism. The idea is the same: Transport air laden with water vapor to high altitudes where the water vapor can condense out to form water droplets. This time, however, the water vapor does not rise because of warming of the surrounding air, but because of getting a running start up a convenient slope.

In orographic lifting, the air containing the water vapor is moving horizontally across the surface due to low-level winds. This parcel of air then encounters the slope of a mountain or other geographic feature. Air has mass and mass in motion has momentum, so when the moving moist air mass encounters a slope, it rises, cooling as it increases in altitude. Eventually, the air parcel is transported to the condensation level, forming a cloud.

The final mechanism employed for transporting moist air to its condensation level is *dynamic lifting*. The principle is the same as that of orographic lifting, except instead of moving up a geographic feature, a warm air mass moves up the slope of a colder air mass. There are a couple of ways in which two moving air masses of different temperatures can interact to transport the warmer air mass to a higher altitude.

Given two equal masses of air, one warm and one cold, the colder air mass is compressed by gravity because of its lower kinetic energy—this compression increases its density in comparison with the warmer air mass. When we set the mass of cold air in motion toward a stationary warmer air mass, the cold air mass pushes its way underneath the warmer air due to this density difference. The blunt edge of the cold air mass acts as a snow plow and very quickly transports the warm air to high altitudes.

When a warmer air mass moves toward a stationary or slower moving cold air mass, the warmer air is less dense than the colder air, so it cannot shove its way under the cold air. Instead, the warm air mass very slowly rises to its condensation level by climbing on top of the colder air mass. Because the leading edge of the warm air mass is not as blunt as that of the cold air mass, the warm air is not transported to its condensation level as quickly—the warm air may move horizontally several hundred miles before it attains the proper altitude.

An additional important factor in the formation of clouds is air stability. When air passes over solar heated land or water, it becomes unstable. The air closest to the ground becomes heated, and it rises to form clouds by way of the convective process already described. However, in a stable air condition, the heavier cold air is underneath warmer air. This can occur, for instance, when ground or water loses heat during the night and cools the air with which it is in contact. This situation is referred to as an inversion, because it is the inverse of the normal situation in which warm air is beneath cooler air.

A temperature inversion effectively cuts off any convection in the lower-altitude cold air mass, making the air very calm and still. Inverted, stable air masses are quite common in cold, wintry regions and over small bodies of water near dawn. A temperature inversion is the reason lakes appear calm and quiet during early morning hours: There is very little air motion in the nonconvective cold air mass to generate waves in the lake.

When the atmosphere is in this condition, it is considered *stratified* because there are two distinct layers, or strata, in the local air situation. Where the cold air and the warm air meet in this stratified condition, the temperature may approach the dew point, and a thin stratus cloud may form along the boundary if the warm air contains enough moisture.

If there is a small breeze or a gentle stirring wind in an inversion condition, moist air in the warm strata might come in contact with the cooled ground. If this happens, the moist air is almost immediately transported to its dew point temperature, and a ground-level stratus cloud, or *fog*, can form. Under the right conditions, fog can reach a thickness of almost 100 meters. When the morning sun raises the ground temperature, the air temperature will rise above its dew point temperature and the fog will dissipate as the water returns to vapor.

Cloud Formation via Convection and Orographic Lifting

Convection

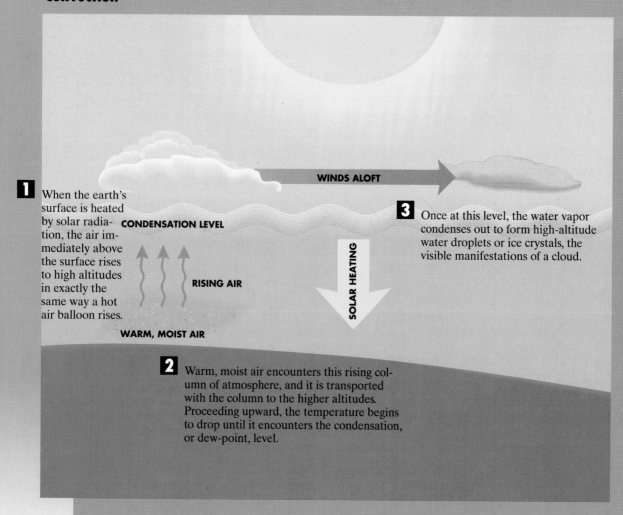

1 When the earth's surface is heated by solar radiation, the air immediately above the surface rises to high altitudes in exactly the same way a hot air balloon rises.

WINDS ALOFT

CONDENSATION LEVEL

RISING AIR

SOLAR HEATING

3 Once at this level, the water vapor condenses out to form high-altitude water droplets or ice crystals, the visible manifestations of a cloud.

WARM, MOIST AIR

2 Warm, moist air encounters this rising column of atmosphere, and it is transported with the column to the higher altitudes. Proceeding upward, the temperature begins to drop until it encounters the condensation, or dew-point, level.

Orographic Lifting

3 As during convection, the warm air cools as altitude increases. Eventually, the water vapor condenses out to water droplets or ice crystals, forming a cloud.

CONDENSATION LEVEL

2 Air has mass, and mass in motion has momentum, so when it encounters a slope such as a mountain or a cold air mass, it continues to travel up the face of the slope.

1 Warm, moist air travels parallel to the surface of the earth, pushed by an approaching storm or high-pressure winds.

WARM, MOIST AIR

Satellite Image of Cloud Formation via Orographic Lifting

Breezes bring warm, moisture-laden air off the Mediterrranean Sea inland into Lebanon. The temperature of the land mass keeps the air warm as it continues its eastward course. As it encounters the mountains, the air rises along the slope, forming cloud masses when the condensation level is reached. Cloud formations can clearly be seen lining the mountain ridges.

Cloud Classification Based on Types and Altitudes

Clouds are classified according to the processes that lead to their formation, their current state, and the altitude of their bases. The cloud types listed here are only the main classifications. Variations based on supplementary features, other formation processes, peculiarities in shape, and strangeness of internal structure result in several dozen additional cloud types, such as stratoformis, congestus, and mammatocumulus.

Typical Cloud Types

CUMULONIMBUS

The base of the cumulus cloud is flat, and indicates the condensation altitude where the cloud has formed from rising moist air. The tops of the cumulus clouds are puffy or bumpy due to internal convection. Although the tops, or towers, of these clouds can rise a great distance into the sky, the base of cumulus clouds begin at an altitude of about 6,000 feet and, as such, are classified as low level. Cumulus clouds are normally separated from each other by noticeable distances, and are in evidence during fair weather.

CUMULUS

Stratus clouds are flat, low-layer clouds that appear in sheets or layers across the sky. Although the width of a stratus cloud may be 10 to 500 miles, the height of the cloud may be only less than a mile. There is no internal convection in a stratus cloud, giving it a wispy, ethereal appearance. A fog bank is a very low-level stratus cloud.

STRATUS

High-level clouds (20,000 feet and greater) have base heights greater than 20,000 feet. Most clouds at this level are formed from ice crystals rather than water droplets because of the extreme low temperatures at these altitudes. High-level clouds include cirrostratus, cirrocumulus and cirrus.

20,000 FT

Middle-level clouds (6,000 to 20,000 feet) have base heights within the 6,000-to-20,000 foot range. Clouds in transition from one state to another (such as cumulus to cumulonimbus) are often found at this level. Middle-level clouds also include altostratus and altocumulus.

6,000 FT

Low-level clouds (0 to 6,000 feet) have *base heights* (the distance from the ground to the base of the cloud) within the 0-to-6,000 foot range. Clouds in this range include stratus, nimbostratus, stratocumulus and cumulus. Many stratocumulus and cumulus clouds can be transported to middle or high levels by aloft winds.

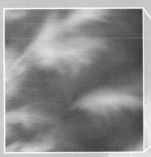

CIRROCUMULUS

CIRROSTRATUS

CIRRUS

Cirrus clouds are beautiful, high-level, wispy structures that are usually composed of ice crystals rather than water droplets. Although these are often precipitating clouds, the precipitation rarely makes it down to the lower altitudes, evaporating instead at the higher altitudes. Ice crystals in the cirrus clouds are responsible for the bright, easily visible halos surrounding the sun or the moon. The light from the sun or the moon is refracted by the ice crystals in the cirrus clouds, forming the halo. These halos normally apear at a distance of either 22° of arc or 46° of arc from the light source. Cirrus clouds often travel in advance of the warm front ahead of a storm system.

ALTOSTRATUS

ALTOCUMULUS

STRATOCUMULUS

Nimbus is a way of describing cloud types that have begun or are beginning the precipitation process. Nimbus clouds are generally dark and brooding in appearance and indicate either precipitation or the approach of precipitation. Because nimbus clouds are indicative of storms, they usually advance along with the storm front, and are often observed racing along at great speeds.

NIMBOSTRATUS

Dance of the Planets

AT THE END OF the sixteenth century and into the seventeenth century, a war was being waged. The goal was nothing short of the conquest of the human mind, and the battlefield was the scientific Renaissance leading Western Europe out of the Middle Ages. The soldiers on one side of the battle line were the religious and government leaders fighting to keep human beings, specifically men, at their "rightful place" at the Center of the Universe. On the other side of the battle were the lone men and women who, with courage and reason their only weapons, looked into the face of nature and saw the world as it is and dared to speak.

In 1609, Johannes Kepler postulated three laws of motion that helped change the way humans look at their planet. The first law stated that planetary orbits in a *heliocentric*, or sun-centered, solar system are not perfect circles, but rather ellipses with the sun placed at one of the foci. Kepler's second law tells us that a planet in such an orbit does not move at a constant velocity, but rather moves faster when it is closer to the sun. The varying speed of motion is such that a planet sweeps across equal areas of the ellipse in equal time regardless of the position of that planet. The third law tells us that the ratio of the average distance of a planet to the sun over the square of the planet's period is the same, no matter what distance the planet is from the sun.

The amount of sunlight that streams down onto the surface of the earth is dependent partially on the complex dance between the earth and the sun; the rules of which were stated so elegantly nearly 400 years ago. When Earth is closest to the sun, its total energy received from our star is 6% to 7% greater than the energy it receives at the other end of the orbit. At first glance, this alone would seem to explain the difference in temperatures from season to season. During the summer, it is logical to assume that we are at the closest approach to the sun, and during the winter, the farthest.

Upon closer examination, however, Kepler's laws fail to explain some basic observed facts. The seasonal variation of temperatures at any given point in time is not uniform across the globe: When it is summer in Seattle, it is winter in Sydney. Also, Kepler's second law tells us that Earth should be moving faster when it is closest to the sun, yet in the Northern Hemisphere, there are more days in summer than there are in winter.

Since Kepler's time, more has come to be realized about Earth's motions through the heavens. Although our distance from the sun is an important factor in the amount of power that the sun imparts to the surface of the earth, it is not the overwhelming factor. On the premise that "nothing is perfect," when the planets finally came into being from their austere beginnings inside the accretion disk, planetary bombardments and other forces prevented their axes of rotation from being perpendicular to the plane of their orbit. Of all the planets in our solar system, only Mercury has an axis lined up nice and neat. At the other extreme, the planet Uranus's rotational axis is tilted 98° to a line perpendicular to its orbital plane. Uranus is literally tipped on its side.

The tilt of Earth's axis of rotation is not nearly as exaggerated as that of Uranus, the inclination being only 23.5° to a line perpendicular to the plane of our orbit. This tilt, combined with our orbital path, completes most of the picture of how we receive energy from our star. The tilt is such that at *aphelion*, the point in our orbit farthest from the sun, the north end of our rotational axis points toward the sun, and at *perihelion*, the point in our orbit closest to the sun, the south end of our rotational axis points toward the sun.

When time is given to consider the geometry of this situation, the seasonal cycles as well as the increasingly cold climate become apparent when traveling north or south from the equator. During the summer season in the Northern Hemisphere, Earth is actually near its aphelion. However, the axis of Earth is pointing toward the direction of the source of heat. Thinking about the light from the sun reaching Earth in parallel beams while Earth is in this configuration, it can be imagined that the Northern Hemisphere receives more direct sunlight than the Southern Hemisphere, which is experiencing winter. Likewise, the situation is reversed when Earth is at perihelion.

During spring and autumn, the transitional seasons, the earth is situated so that neither the Northern or Southern Hemisphere is favored, and the result is nearly uniform heating between opposing latitudes, that is, the amount of sunlight received at 40° North latitude is roughly the same as the amount of sunlight received at 40° South latitude. Remember that the Southern Hemisphere is experiencing its winter at the aphelion and its summer at the perihelion, and as such, either 6% less solar energy in the winter or 6% more solar energy in the summer. In other words, the Southern Hemisphere should have colder winters and hotter summers than does the Northern Hemisphere. The increase in solar energy, however, is offset by the greater amount of water in the Southern Hemisphere. The higher heat capacity, or energy required to raise the temperature of a substance, of water has a moderating effect on the temperature in the Southern Hemisphere.

The view from the earth reflects this interplay between the tilt of the earth's axis and its position from the sun. Considering only the Northern Hemisphere for the moment, Earth reaches its aphelion on June 21, known as the summer solstice. At this point, the sun reaches its highest angle in the sky and the Northern Hemisphere receives its greatest amount of solar heating. On June 21 at latitude 23.5° North, the same angle that Earth's axis is tilted from its orbital plane, the sun would be directly overhead at noon. Conversely, at the date of Earth's perihelion, December 21 or the winter solstice, the Northern Hemisphere receives the least amount of solar input. At exactly these same dates in the Southern Hemisphere, the opposite is occurring: The Southern Hemisphere receives the greatest amount of heat on December 21, and the least amount on June 21.

Because of the curvature of the earth, the rays of the sun strike the surface of our planet at an increasing oblique angle the closer you are to the poles. The more oblique the angle, the less energy absorbed by the earth and the cooler the average temperature. This implies that the amount of energy received on average at 40° North latitude is more than the amount of energy received at 50° North latitude at any given time. This heat differential causes energy to be transferred from warmer areas to cooler ones in part due to thermal convection.

The laws of thermal convection state that when a gas is heated, its density is decreased. This causes the gas to rise and be replaced by cooler surrounding gas. This cooler gas is also heated and also rises. The process that ensues produces a convection current. If the situation were left to thermal convection alone, all of the atmosphere would collect at the equator. However, there is an imbalance in horizontal pressure that is created aloft by the air piling up at the equator due to convection. This pressure imbalance causes the air aloft to flow back towards the poles. These convection currents are an important component of the weather machine, and they will be talked about in greater detail in later chapters. For now, it's sufficient that we have laid the groundwork for the basic principle of thermal input to Earth's weather system.

The Seasons and Their Relationship to Earth's Orbit

September 22, autumnal equinox in the Northern Hemisphere
At this point in the orbit, neither axes are inclined toward the sun. In theory, opposing latitudes should be receiving equal energy and the length of daylight should be the same. The Northern Hemisphere is preparing to enter winter.

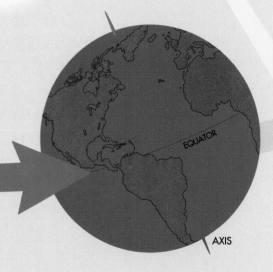

SUN

147.1 MILLION KM

Perihelion: December 21, winter solstice in the Northern Hemisphere The North Pole of the planet is inclined 23° 27' from a line perpendicular to the plane of the orbit. At this point in our orbit, the northernmost part of the axis is tilted *away* from the sun, causing the Southern Hemisphere to receive the majority of the sun's heat. The days are shorter than the nights in the Northern Hemisphere. In fact, any point on the globe within the circle described by 66° 33' North latitude, also called the Arctic Circle, does not receive sunlight. An observer at 23° 27' South latitude will notice the sun directly overhead at noon on this day.

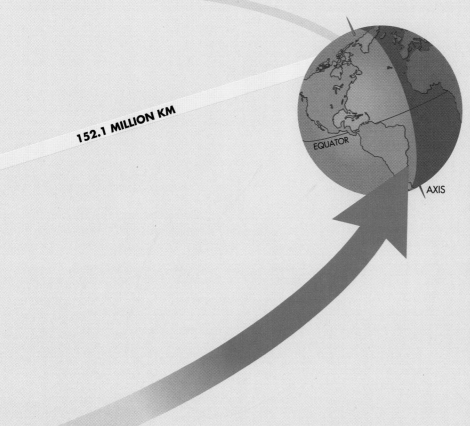

152.1 MILLION KM

EQUATOR

AXIS

Aphelion: June 21, summer solstice in the Northern Hemisphere The northernmost part of our axis is pointing at the sun, and the situation is reversed from what occurs at perihelion. Now the Northern Hemisphere is receiving the vast majority of solar energy, and in fact is currently receiving more solar input during a single day than it will receive at any other point in its orbit. The Southern Hemisphere has more darkness than light. An observer at 23° 27' North latitude will notice the sun directly overhead at noon on this day.

March 20, vernal equinox in the Northern Hemisphere Like the autumnal equinox, Earth is at a point in its orbit where the sun is not favoring either axis. The length of days and energy input should be the same on opposing latitudes. The Northern Hemisphere is shedding winter and preparing to enter into summer.

Sunlight Arriving at Earth on June 21

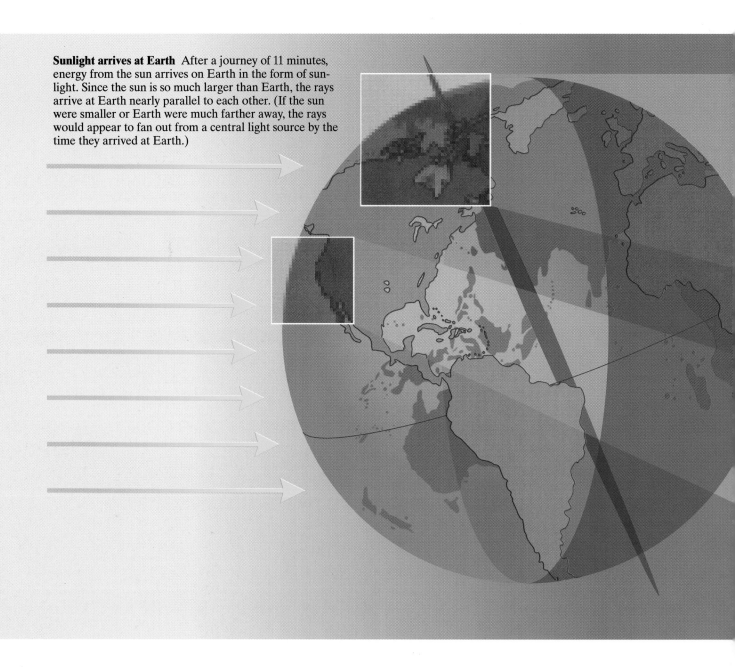

Sunlight arrives at Earth After a journey of 11 minutes, energy from the sun arrives on Earth in the form of sunlight. Since the sun is so much larger than Earth, the rays arrive at Earth nearly parallel to each other. (If the sun were smaller or Earth were much farther away, the rays would appear to fan out from a central light source by the time they arrived at Earth.)

All things are not equal Due to the curvature of the earth, the sunlight strikes the surface at increasingly oblique angles as you travel farther north. The relationship between the angles highlighted is $x > y > z$. As this implies, the energy received at point A is greater than the energy received at point B or C. For this reason, the temperature decreases in general the farther north or south one gets from the equator.

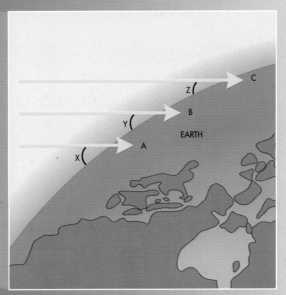

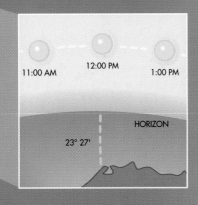

High noon On this date, an observer at latitude $23°\ 27'$ North would see the sun straight overhead at precisely 12:00 noon. This is because the inclination of Earth's axis is $23°\ 27'$ from a line perpendicular to the plane of Earth's orbit, called the ecliptic. So, at this date, a line perpendicular to the surface of the earth at $23°\ 27'$ North latitude would lie directly in the ecliptic.

Absorption of Solar Radiation

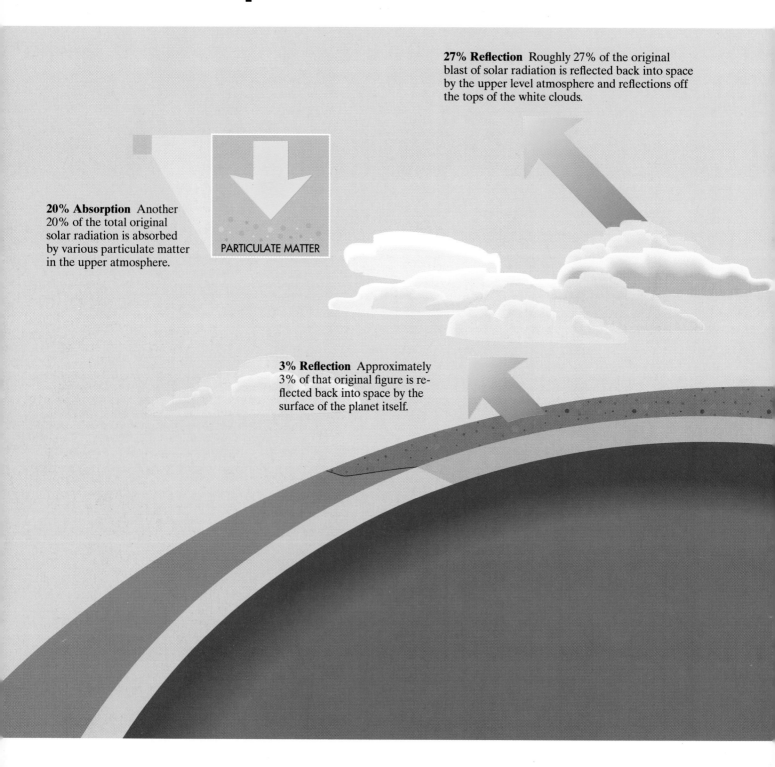

27% Reflection Roughly 27% of the original blast of solar radiation is reflected back into space by the upper level atmosphere and reflections off the tops of the white clouds.

20% Absorption Another 20% of the total original solar radiation is absorbed by various particulate matter in the upper atmosphere.

PARTICULATE MATTER

3% Reflection Approximately 3% of that original figure is reflected back into space by the surface of the planet itself.

100% pure energy At an idealized point on the earth's surface where the sunlight is perpendicular to the surface of the planet (such as 23° 27' North latitude on June 21), the top of the atmosphere receives a full dose of solar radiation. This will be our benchmark measurement of 100% energy.

EARTH'S SURFACE

50% Absorption Of the original amount of sunlight, a full 50% makes it to the surface to be absorbed by the land and the sea. This energy is a crucial component in the normal functioning of the Earth's *greenhouse effect*, the reradiation of the absorbed energy as long-wave energy. This reemitted radiation is absorbed by the atmosphere and helps drive winds, form clouds, and warm the surface of the earth. In addition, the energy absorbed by the earth is responsible for a process called heat lag. The planet is constantly absorbing solar energy, but at periods of lessened solar energy (late afternoon, nighttime), there is a net heat loss, so the reradiation of the energy becomes more apparent. Heat lag is responsible for effects such as the hottest part of the day occurring a few hours after the sun has reached its highest elevation, as well as the hottest part of the summer occurring long after the solstice.

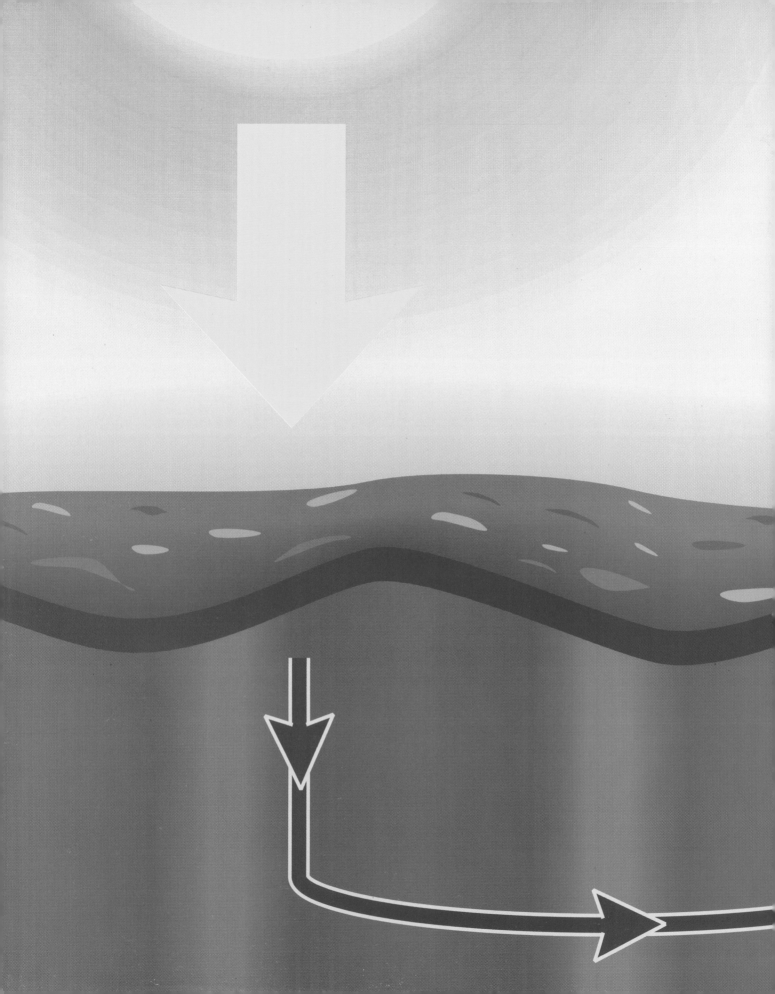

THE SOURCE OF POWER

CONTENTS

W E KNOW THAT the atmosphere has depth and structure; we can examine and label its various layers as we do the layers of a cliff face. A cross-section of the strata shows that each layer is at once very similar and very different from the one just above or below. As we progress downward through this soup of air, we arrive at the floor of a complex, highly active ocean of gas that began 5 billion years in the past. Yet the earth has not sat around like a 5-billion-year-old cesspool allowing gases to settle to their natural buoyancy levels.

Our atmospheric system has remained far from stagnant. The most visible manifestations of these dynamic processes include water vapor moving through the air for hundreds or thousands of miles, storm systems raging at places as geographically diverse as Texas and Tibet, and the 10,000, or so, lightning strikes occurring around the globe at any given moment. We exist inside of a giant weather machine.

Perhaps it would be more accurate to state that we are a *part* of that machine, since everything that humans do affects the earth in some fashion. The existence of 5.5 billion humans milling about the surface of the planet touches everything from wind patterns to atmospheric content. Humans, however, are only small cogs in our weather machine. Winds move topsoil and water, giant storm systems change the landscape of the planet, and seasons change in ready, predictable cycles. These events were occurring long before we appeared on the scene in numbers great enough to have an effect.

As there is no such thing as perpetual motion, it stands to reason that something external to our atmosphere is powering this machine. Heat trapped from the original creation of the planet and heat that is still being generated by radioactive decay continues to form our world. Internal heat moves continents, forms new land, warms the ocean from below, and provides energy for geysers. Although this internal heat mostly accounts for the dynamics of earth's geology, it also continues the process of *outgassing*, adding new gases to our atmosphere through volcanic eruptions and heat vents. These new gases change our atmospheric content and density and, thereby, alter the dynamics of the atmospheric system. These changes, however, can only be noted to take effect over long periods of time: hundreds or thousands of years. Where does the power for the constant, day-to-day weather activity come from?

To answer this question, look straight up toward our sun. Energy, in the form of heat, reaches us via radiative transfer from this giant, glowing fusion reactor. An average of 300 watts of heat energy per square foot arrives on the surface of our planet every second. We have already described how moist air blowing over sun-warmed ground is a catalyst for cloud making, but this solar heat differential contributes to most of the atmospheric dynamics, from seasonal cycles to hurricane formation.

Earth may be humankind's cradle, but it's the sun that makes it rock.

Atmosphere-Ocean Interaction

OVER TWO-THIRDS OF the earth's surface is covered in water. Oceans, lakes, rivers, and seas make up a surprising portion of our planet's surface area. Although there is evidence that Mars had free-flowing water in its past, and Europa, one of the Galilean moons of Jupiter, is probably all liquid water underneath its surface-covering skin of ice, no other planet or satellite in our solar system presently has as much free-flowing water as does Earth.

Earth is in a unique place in the solar system; it occupies an orbit that allows for the existence of water in all of its phase states: solid, liquid, and gas. Because the temperature range of these states is so narrow, the number of possible positions for a planetary orbit that allows them all to exist is very small. This orbital range is sometimes chauvinistically referred to as the "biotorus," implying that life cannot exist outside of these orbital parameters. One fact is certain, however: The abundance of water on our planet has a profound influence on our weather. The atmosphere and the oceans constantly transfer energy between each other, and most of the storm systems, air mass movement, and planetary heat conditions would be impossible without this energy dance.

Transport of water via cloud formations is not the only manner in which our water system affects the weather. Our oceans and seas are responsible for distributing energy around the planet, as well as for storing that energy throughout the year. It is important to understand that in the physical world, one of the ways that energy is manifest is in the presence of heat, which is generally regarded as the average kinetic energy (or all possible physical motions) of the molecules that make up a substance. The study of the nature of heat and its conversion into other energy forms is called thermodynamics.

Other than a concept to express among humans, there is no such thing as cold in the physical world, there is only the lack of heat. Although this seems like a matter of semantics, it is not. These varying temperatures around us are really measurements of the flow of heat from one substance to another substance, in accordance with the three laws of thermodynamics. When your body feels cold in the winter, it is because the surrounding air and radiant solar temperature is such that heat energy is being transferred from your body to the air around you. Heat energy is leaving your system, and you perceive this transfer of energy as cold.

There are three ways in which heat energy is transferred in the physical universe: *conduction, convection,* and *radiation.* The first method, *conduction,* is the transmission of heat energy through physical contact. Placing a hot water bottle next to your skin will transfer heat energy from the hot water bottle to you. In an ideal system, the total heat energy of the hot water bottle will decrease and the total heat energy of your skin will increase until they are equal.

The transmission of heat via the flow of a liquid or gas through a like medium is known as *convection.* A current of hot water running through a cool stream will transfer energy to that stream. Likewise, rising warm air transfers energy to cooler air above it. If the rising warm air is replaced by cool air, and the source of heat continues, a convection cell is established.

Finally, *radiation* is the transfer of energy via either electromagnetic or particle waves. Radiative transfer does not require a medium to transport it, only the wave itself. In fact, the presence of a medium can actually hamper radiative transfer of energy. This is how energy is efficiently imparted to Earth from the sun through the relative void of space.

Soil and rock do a particularly poor job of storing heat energy. Convection is not really possible in solid rock (although it does occur in molten rock), and radiative transfer is inefficient through this material. This leaves conduction as the main energy-transfer mechanism, and solid rock and soil are not very good at that, either. Typical energy transfer depths are only about one meter, and even over the course of a year, the energy only reaches down a few meters. (This is one of the reasons that the internal heat energy of the planet has not been significantly reduced over 4.5 billion years; the amount of energy being lost via thermal conduction is less than the amount of energy added to the system due to internal pressures and natural nuclear radiation.)

Heat absorbed by the earth is not stored then, but is reradiated back into the system at longer wavelengths almost immediately, obtaining a nearly zero net-sum gain over a year's seasonal variation. This poor heat-storage capacity is the reason the surface of the planet bounces back so rapidly from each seasonal change in the higher latitudes. Even though the earth is subjected to quite a bit of solar radiation over the summer, it does not maintain that heat in the winter months, and it does not take much springtime sunlight to reheat the soil and revive the plants and animals that lie dormant beneath.

By contrast, the oceans are an amazing heat sink, storing the heat by redistributing the energy through its depths via convection. Energy information is transferred to depths of a few hundred meters; since its heat capacity is higher than that of the land, it heats up and cools off much more slowly. In addition, energy transfer in bodies of water is not limited to straight up-and-down, or vertical, transfer. The oceans, for example, have underwater streams and rivers that are analogous to the atmosphere's jet streams. These underwater currents can transfer energy for thousands of miles, redistributing the heat throughout the ocean.

The effect of this redistribution is apparent to anyone living in a coastal or near-coastal city. Because the underwater oceanic currents tend to move east to west, the eastern seaboard of each continent is warmer than the corresponding western seaboard of that continent at the same latitude. The coastal waters off Washington, D.C., for instance, are an average 2.8°C to 5.6°C (5°F to 10°F) warmer than the waters off San Francisco. Energy absorbed in the middle of the Atlantic is transferred via convection to the eastern U.S. seaboard, and energy absorbed in the waters off the western U.S. is transported out into the Pacific.

The result of the increased heat capacity of water is obvious in the higher latitudes in the winter. A –2.2°C (28°F) day 20 miles west of Boston may bring snow, while in Boston, the temperature is 0.6°C (33°F) and it's raining. The overall air temperature near Boston has been increased by the warmer, ocean-fed air. The farther west you go from Boston, the more the temperature drops.

Other forms of energy transfer that do not involve heat also take place between the atmosphere and the ocean. The motion of the atmosphere at lower altitudes imparts direct kinetic energy to the surface of the water, causing swells and wave activity. This wave motion can vary from small whitecaps on lakes to large, powerful waves many feet in height. This wave energy can travel many hundreds of miles through deep water, its speed based on the depth of the water and the gravitational pull of the earth. When the energy approaches shallower water, the energy takes on the form of a wave crest, expending all of its internal energy rather quickly. This is visible as the wave breaks on or near the shore.

Experiments are now taking place to try to harness some of this wave energy for electric power in coastal regions and island nations. Britain, for instance, has an experiment underway involving a string of wave dampers, many miles long, to catch the waves as they break and translate their wave energy to mechanical energy, which can then be stored and reused.

Energy Absorption and Redistribution by the Oceans

In the colder latitudes, sunlight does not fall on the ocean as directly or continuously as it does in the equatorial region. In these areas, more energy is radiated out annually than is absorbed. One source of the energy is sunlight that was absorbed in the equatorial regions and transported to the colder latitudes via subocean currents.

These contour lines represent the average annual energy absorbed (positive values) or emitted (negative values) by the Atlantic ocean. The values are in watts per square meter.

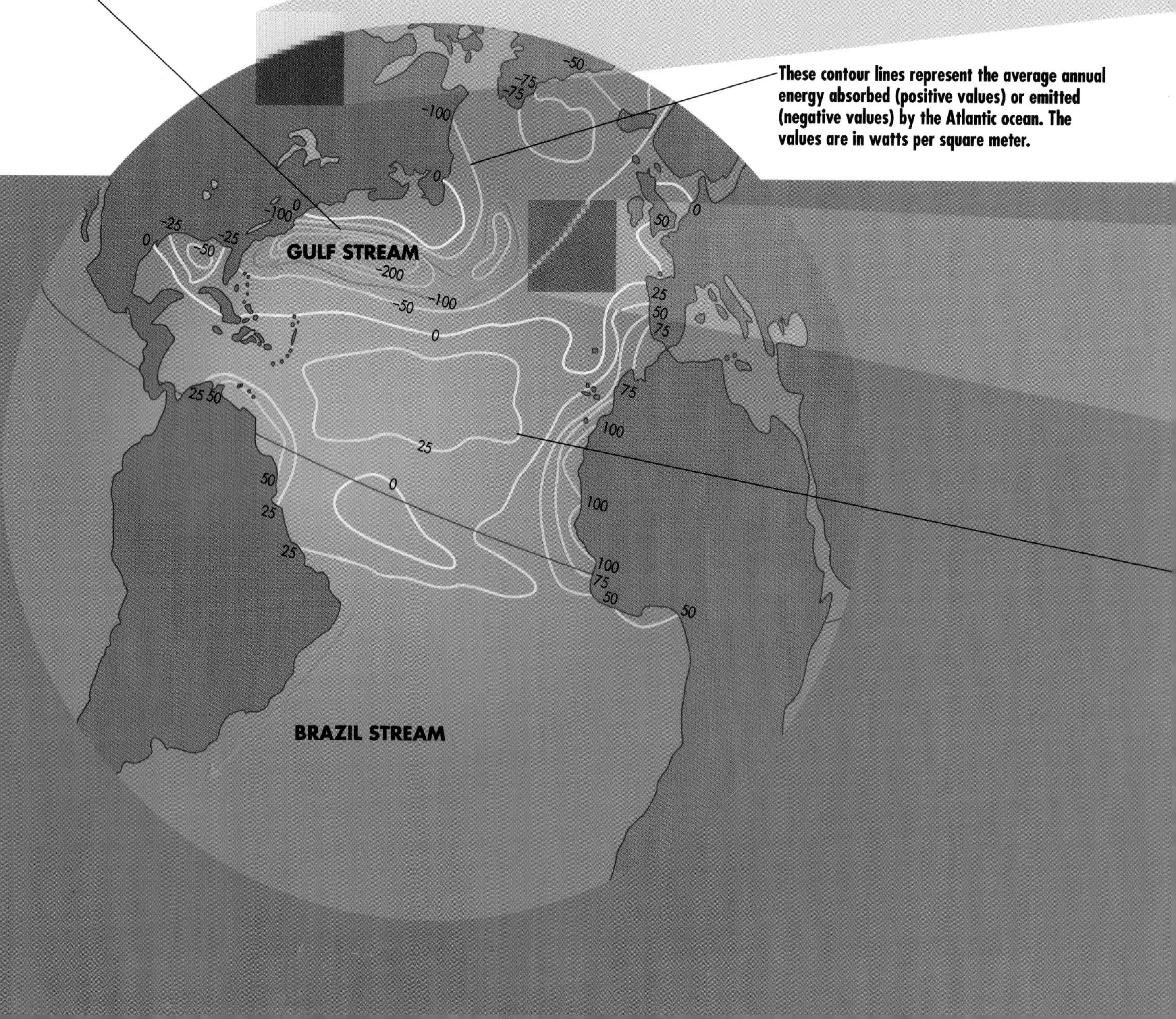

GULF STREAM

BRAZIL STREAM

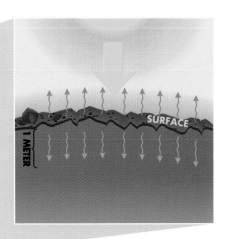

The same amount of energy that falls on water also falls on a land mass. Rock and soil are poor heat sinks, since convection transfer of heat through rock is impossible in solid rock, and radiative transfer of heat through rock is very difficult. Slow, conductive heat moves the heat downwards only a few meters. The heat is almost immediately reradiated in longer wavelengths back into the atmosphere.

Energy in the form of solar radiation falls on the ocean. The heat energy is submerged many hundreds of meters deep into the ocean due to convective action. The heated water is then transported via strong underwater currents to other locations, sometimes many thousands of kilometers away.

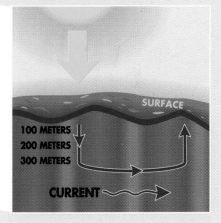

The equatorial region of the globe receives the most amount of continual, direct sunlight. As such, it absorbs the most energy, with between 25 and 100 watts of energy per square meter being absorbed downward via convective action. Part of this heat energy is stored in the ocean for long periods of time, while part of it is transported to colder regions via underwater currents.

Earth Dance—The Earth's Rotation and Atmospheric Mixing

THE EARTH'S AIR blanket is quite susceptible to changes in energy input from the sun. Moist air, warmed by the sun, rises until it reaches its condensation temperature, at which point clouds form. Vertical towers of convection cells can be achieved by placing cold air over a heated surface: The warm air rises and is replaced by cooler air, which then warms up and also rises. As the warm column of air gets higher, it cools off and begins to sink to where it is warmed again. These localized temperature changes affect the vertical motion of the atmosphere. This explains the rising and falling of air masses, but does it explain the motion of the air across the surface of the planet?

All in all, the vertical component of air motion is relatively small when compared with the horizontal component, commonly referred to as wind. Although it does occur, rare is the instance when air rockets upwards or downwards at speeds of 20, 30, or 40 miles per hour. Horizontal winds, however, routinely hit these velocities, and in some instances, can obtain speeds of over 100 miles an hour. How does air move parallel to the ground?

If Earth were a featureless globe that did not rotate and was heated equally over every square kilometer, in all likelihood there would be little atmospheric motion. Fortunately, we live on a planet—covered with oceans, mountains, and ice—which is spinning on its axis once every 24 hours, exposing different parts of its surface to a single source of heat. There are several factors involved in atmospheric circulation, but the two main forces are uneven heating of the surface of the earth at different latitudes and the rotation of the earth about its axis. It would be most convenient to discuss these as two separate topics, but in creating our model of global circulation patterns, they are inexorably linked.

Consider the following illustration "The Six Major Air Circulation Cells." The image represents the position of Earth with respect to the sun on June 21, the point farthest from the sun and the beginning of summer in the Northern Hemisphere and of winter in the Southern Hemisphere. Imagine for the moment that Earth did not rotate about a common axis and that the position of Earth to the sun was fairly constant. In this arrested state, it is obvious that uneven heating is still occurring. The equatorial regions absorb the majority of the sunlight, and the polar regions receive only a fraction of that energy, since the sunlight strikes the surface at an oblique angle.

In this situation, the global air circulation patterns would not be hard to imagine. The surface of the earth near the equator would be heated, causing the air in the vicinity to rise. Nature abhors a vacuum, so cooler air would rush in to take the place of the warm air. The cooler air would in turn be heated, and a large convection cell would be established. The air that was transported via heating to the higher altitudes would travel either northward or southward, depending on which hemisphere it was in. As the air approached the cooler, high-latitude regions, the air would sink and enter the convection cell at the bottom.

Earth, however, does rotate about a common axis, and the amount of sunlight that each region receives varies from season to season, so the picture is quite a bit more complicated. In the early part of the nineteenth century, Gaspard Coriolis developed a mathematical principle to describe the motion of objects relative to a noninertial, uniformly rotating frame of reference such as Earth. His principle was given the name *Coriolis Force*—a bit of a misnomer, since the effect is not really a force, but a trick of reference frames that appears to an observer to be an unseen force.

The effect can best be described as follows: Earth rotates from west to east, so an object wishing to travel in a straight course from the North Pole to the equator will be subjected to Earth rotating out from underneath it. The end result is that the object will wind up west of its intended destination. To an outside observer, it appears as though the object has a gently curving westward course. The effect is more pronounced, the closer a moving object is to the equator. Similarly, an object moving to the north from the equator would appear to drift eastward. The rule of thumb is that in the Northern Hemisphere, objects drift to the right of the direction of motion; in the Southern Hemisphere, objects drift to the left.

The effects of the Coriolis Force are a part of everyday life: In the Northern Hemisphere, planes drift slightly to the right and so must constantly be correcting their course; north-south train tracks tend to wear out on the right rail first; and rivers first erode the right side of their banks. The atmosphere is also subjected to this mysterious force, and northern winds tend to become northeastern winds during their travels.

In 1735, an English barrister turned meteorologist, George Hadley, proposed a theory to explain the northeastern trade winds between the equator and roughly $30°$ North latitude. Hadley suggested that a northerly wind caused by falling air around the $30°$ mark would actually blow out of the Northeast toward the Southwest because of the rotation of Earth.

His ideas were ridiculed and shelved until 1793, when an English mathematician and physical sciences professor at Manchester college backed up Hadley's idea with that of Gaspard Coriolis. The end result was the theory, and later discovery, of a series of six major circulation cells encircling the globe. The Northern Hemisphere has the Hadley Cell from the equator to 30° N latitude, the Ferrel Cell from 30° N to 60° N, and the Polar Cell from 60° N to 90° N. The Southern Hemisphere has three analogous circulation cell regions. These six circulation cells explain a large part of the earth's atmospheric circulation pattern, so let us return to our global model, adjusting for global rotation.

The air in the equatorial region heats up and rises, creating a low pressure area near the equator. The rising air, if it is to the north of the equator, flows northeasterly until it descends around 30° N. latitude, bringing with it warm dry air. After its descent, the air is pulled along by the pressure difference caused by the upwelling air near the equator. Due to the Coriolis effect, it travels from northeast to southwest, forming the northeast trade winds. In the Southern Hemisphere, the analogous cell is circulating, and the northeast trade winds collide with the southeastern trade winds in the low-pressure area formed near the equator. This collision of air masses creates a convergence zone of heavy rainfall. For centuries, sailors have called this region, which lies from 10° S to 10° N latitude, the *doldrums* due to the poor wind speeds.

The next circulation cell in the series rotates in the opposite direction of the Hadley Cell. The high-pressure region in area 30° N latitude (30° S latitude in the Southern Hemisphere) causes the winds to blow from the southwesterly direction, until they rise in the region of 60° N latitude (60° S latitude in the Southern Hemisphere). This middle latitude circulation cell is called the Ferrel Cell.

The final set of cells in the polar regions of the planet returns the flow of the surface winds to a northeast-to-southwest pattern. This upper-latitude Polar Cell is the weakest of the three sets of cells, but has the important job of transferring frigid, arctic air to the middle-latitude zone's Ferrel Cell. This process contributes to maintaining a global energy balance.

The Coriolis Effect

Postulated by Gaspard Coriolis in the nineteenth century, the Coriolis effect is commonly referred to as the Coriolis Force. The effect is not really a force, but a trick of the reference frame of the observer. Consider an object, for instance a plane, is traveling from the North Pole to a destination on the equator. While it is in motion, the earth is rotating out from underneath it. Unless the plane continually corrects its course, it will arrive west of its intended destination. Although this is a simple north-to-south example, the drifting can be observed on any object traveling in any direction over the surface of the globe: to the right in the Northern Hemisphere, and to the left in the Southern Hemisphere.

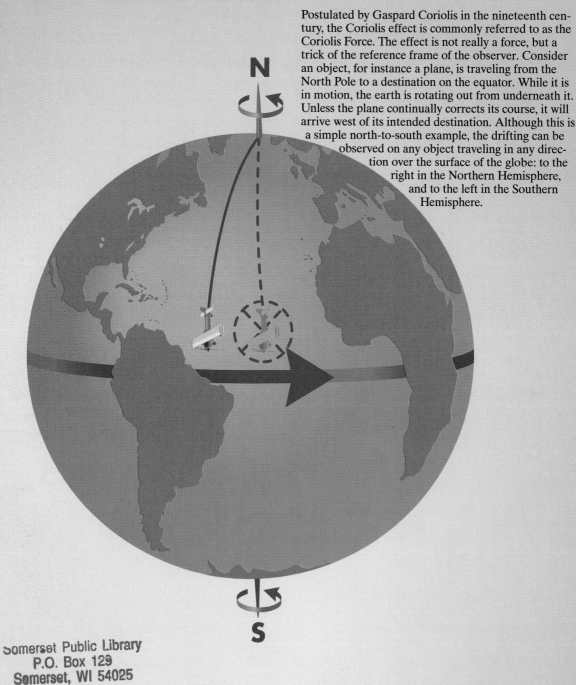

A plane flying in essentially any direction north of the equator will have to continually correct its course to keep from being pushed to starboard, or right. It has the effect of a mysterious force trying to push the plane off course.

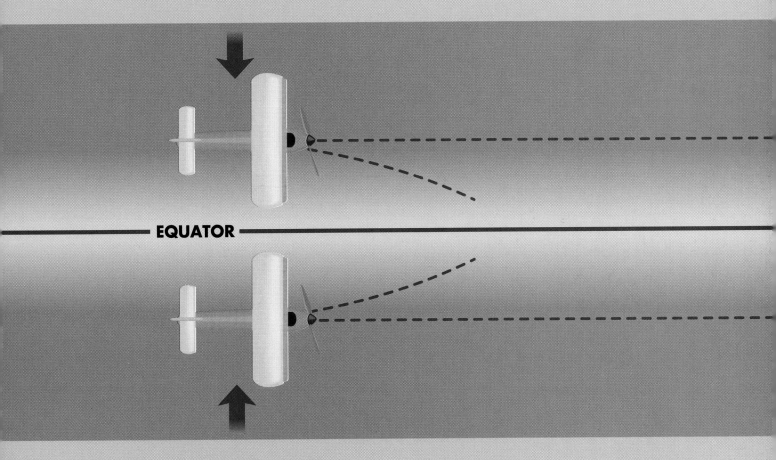

A plane south of the equator experiences a strong "force" pushing it to port, so the plane must correct its course to keep from drifting in that direction.

The Six Major Air Circulation Cells

The Polar Cell is a weaker cell system that brings cold arctic air down to be picked up by the Ferrel Cell for distribution to the mid-latitude regions.

The Ferrel, or Mid-Latitude, Cell transports warm air up to the high-middle latitudes where it is exchanged for cold, arctic air that descends near the 30° latitude range.

The Hadley Cell is formed by heated equatorial air rising and forming a low-pressure system in the latitude range of 10° S to 10° N. The air is transported north until it cools enough for it to sink around the 30° latitude. This creates a high-pressure system.

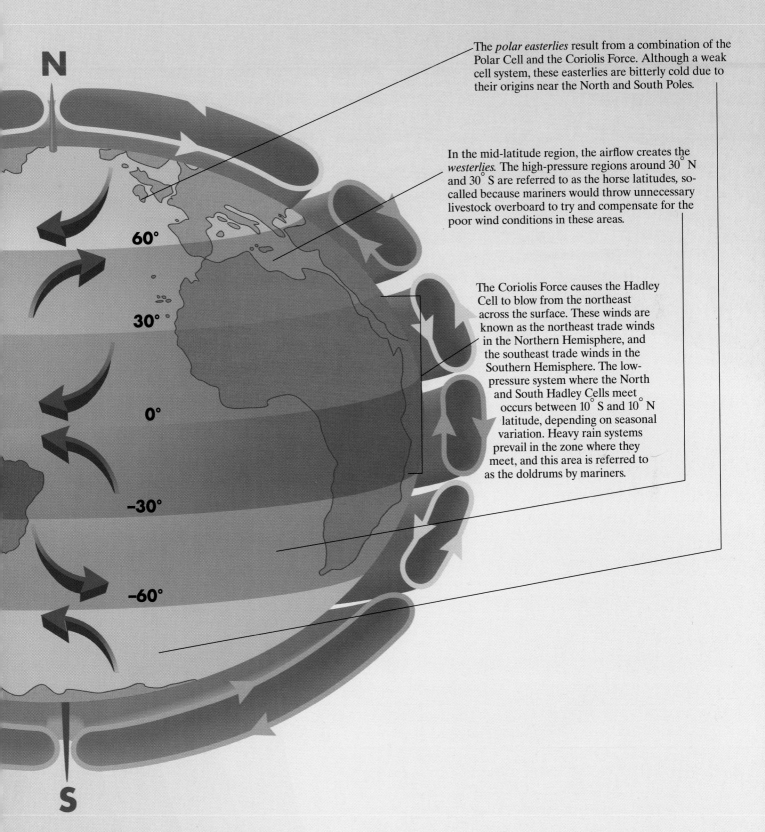

N

The *polar easterlies* result from a combination of the Polar Cell and the Coriolis Force. Although a weak cell system, these easterlies are bitterly cold due to their origins near the North and South Poles.

In the mid-latitude region, the airflow creates the *westerlies.* The high-pressure regions around 30° N and 30° S are referred to as the horse latitudes, so-called because mariners would throw unnecessary livestock overboard to try and compensate for the poor wind conditions in these areas.

The Coriolis Force causes the Hadley Cell to blow from the northeast across the surface. These winds are known as the northeast trade winds in the Northern Hemisphere, and the southeast trade winds in the Southern Hemisphere. The low-pressure system where the North and South Hadley Cells meet occurs between 10° S and 10° N latitude, depending on seasonal variation. Heavy rain systems prevail in the zone where they meet, and this area is referred to as the doldrums by mariners.

60°

30°

0°

-30°

-60°

S

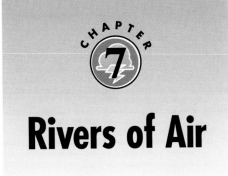

Rivers of Air

COLD AIR IS denser than warm air and has less internal movement. The molecules that make up the air tend to have less kinetic energy. As such, cold air will move towards its gravitational minimum; in other words it will rest near the surface of the earth. If you were to travel upwards in a column of cold air, you would find that the air pressure decreases rapidly with altitude. Again, this is because the majority of the air in the cold column is near the earth's surface.

By contrast, warm air contains energetic molecules that prefer to be anything but stationary. Warm air tends to rise, and the air packets making up a column of warm air do not tend to congregate near the surface. So, if you were to travel upwards in a tower of warm air, you would find that the air pressure decreased much more slowly with altitude than it did in an equivalent column of cold air.

Now, take what we know about pressure differences caused by differing temperatures in different masses of air and apply it to a larger scale. Consider only the Northern Hemisphere for the moment: Pressure differences at high altitudes vary from the north to south latitudes. Upper-altitude (6 to 10 kilometers) air in the equatorial latitudes has higher pressure than does upper-altitude air in the upper latitudes because the air is generally warmer in the equitorial latitudes. The result is that at high altitudes, air tends to flow from the south to the north. When the Coriolis effect is included, this northward wind deviates to the right (or east), creating the prevailing westerlies.

It would be tempting to say that this effect becomes ever more pronounced at greater and greater altitudes. After all, if the pressure gradient at 6 kilometers above the surface is sufficient to cause a north-south air motion of a certain speed, wouldn't the speed be greater at 15 or 20 kilometers above the surface? In a nutshell, the answer is no. Ambient air temperature decreases with the height in the troposphere. In addition, the temperature gradient between higher and lower latitudes decreases with altitude. The result is a decrease in the pressure differences between different latitudes at very high altitudes. This leaves us with a strong westerly wind in the Northern Hemisphere's mid-latitudes (and a strong easterly wind in the Southern Hemisphere's mid-latitudes) that peaks out just below the tropopause.

Pressure gradients due to temperature differentials produce a phenomenon in the atmosphere called a jet stream. Technically, a *jet stream* is a river of air traveling at least 50 knots, or 57.5 miles per hour. In practice, however, they have a considerably higher velocity, with wind speeds of 100 to 150 miles per hour being quite common, with some reports of velocities in the 200 mile per hour range. The rate of airflow inside of the jet stream is dependent on pressure differentials, which in turn are dependent on temperature differentials. So jet streams are the strongest when it is winter in that stream's hemisphere, because it is during the winter that temperature differentials are the most pronounced.

These rivers of air tend to form along long boundaries of warm and cold air masses, which often encircle the globe. However, these streams do not form a great circle along latitudinal lines, but instead tend to dip and rise, forming a sinewy trajectory around the planet. The dip toward the equator is called a trough; the rise toward the polar region is called a ridge. These troughs and ridges vary from week to week and season to season, advancing around the globe as they move farther south or north.

In the winter, the Northern Hemisphere has two main jet streams: the polar jet, typically found along the vicinity of the Canadian/U.S. border, and the subtropical jet over northern Mexico. Aside from giving a boost to eastern-bound aircraft, the jet streams (especially the polar jet) play a fundamental role in driving our weather systems. As the air currents in a jet stream head southward into a trough, the cold air they carry with them tends to drop in altitude. The drop in altitude forces warm air beneath the jet stream downward and increases the local air pressure directly below the stream. Air flows outward from this high-pressure center and, due to the Coriolis effect, the outflow tends to move toward the right, causing a clockwise, or *anticyclonic*, rotation of air. The net effect to residents on the ground is dry, clear weather.

As the air in the jet stream begins its northward trek toward the ridge of the stream, it brings with it the warmer air from the southern latitudes. This air will tend to rise as it enters the colder air of the higher latitudes. This increase in altitude causes a decrease in the local air pressure directly beneath the stream. This low-pressure system causes surrounding air to rush into the vacated space in a vain attempt to equalize the air pressure. Again, the Coriolis effect takes over and the incoming air is steered to the right, forming a counterclockwise, or *cyclonic*, rotational system. In this case, the influx of air drags surrounding warm air into the cyclone, causing it to rise. This process can result in a storm system.

In both cases, the cyclonic or anticyclonic activity produced by the jet stream is steered by the stream itself as the wave formation progresses eastward. A winter storm system caused by a low pressure region, for instance, will be steered across the United States in a roughly easterly or northeasterly direction. On occasion, the trough-ridge wave formation in the jet stream remains nearly stationary for several days. When this occurs, the weather patterns induced by the stream will also remain in place. A hot, humid summer period, for instance, may remain in place for days due to a persistent high-pressure cell, or a winter storm may dump a dozen inches of snow as the low-pressure cell that induced the storm moves slowly out of the region.

One additional property of the jet stream should be noted, because it applies to the way the it supplies itself with atmosphere for continuing its 150-mile-per-hour "breeze." In the 1700s, a Swiss scientist, Daniel Bernoulli, experimentally showed that a fast moving stream of liquid creates a pressure imbalance between its internal pressure and that of any surrounding fluid. In effect, the internal pressure in a fast moving stream decreases as the velocity of the stream increases. This phenomenon is called the Bernoulli effect.

Again, consider a jet stream in the Northern Hemisphere: As the jet stream advances, its internal pressure is lowered. Nature makes an attempt at satisfying this pressure imbalance by providing the stream with more air, the best source of which is from wherever the air pressure is greatest. This increase of air intake gives the stream a higher velocity, which decreases its internal pressure still further. You might be tempted to think this process is self-sustaining (or self-perpetuating!), but it is not. It only helps to amplify the effect of the jet stream. If it were not for the vertical pressure differences between the cold air mass on one side of the stream and the warm air mass on the other, the stream would cease to exist.

Typical Winter Jet Stream Configuration in the Northern Hemisphere

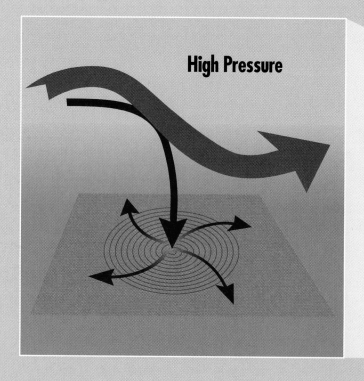

High Pressure

As air in the jet stream enters a trough it begins a drop in altitude, forming a high-pressure cell. Air near the surface is pushed away from the cell, producing an anticyclonic rotation in the atmosphere. High-pressure cells normally mean clear, dry weather.

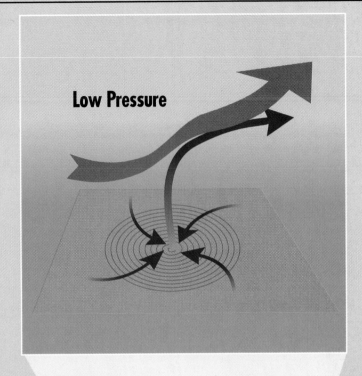

Low Pressure

Cold air masses in the upper latitudes produce lower pressure regions at higher altitudes. Conversely, warm air masses in the equatorial latitudes produce greater air pressure at higher altitudes. These pressure differences in the upper altitudes begin an air flow exchange. The rotation of Earth causes the air to flow in a west-to-east direction. The resultant jet stream commonly has wind speeds between 100 and 150 miles per hour and can sometimes reach speeds over 200 miles per hour.

As the air begins its journey into a ridge, the altitude of the air increases. This causes the atmosphere below the stream to decrease in air pressure, and surrounding air rushes in to try to stabilize the pressure. The result is a cyclonic rotation of air that drags in surrounding air mass. The result can be an increase in warm air for that region, which can produce storm systems. A low-pressure center is normally associated with active weather.

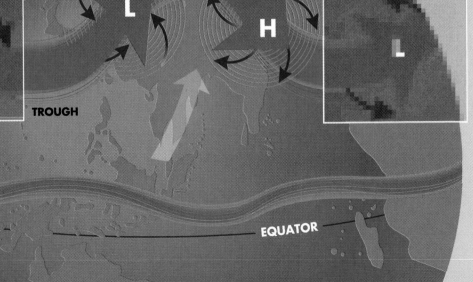

RIDGE

TROUGH

EQUATOR

The Appetite of the Jet Stream

The pressure gradient at upper altitudes, combined with the Coriolis effect, is what calls the jet stream into being. The jet stream is much more active and pronounced during the winter months, because the temperature (and therefore, pressure) difference between air masses in the equatorial latitudes and air masses in the upper latitudes is greater.

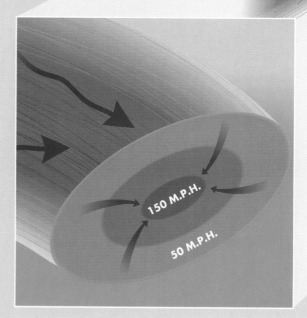

If you were to examine a cross-sectional slice of a jet stream, you would find that air pressure decreased and air stream velocity increased as you got closer to the center. As the jet of air increases in velocity, its internal pressure decreases due to processes described by the Bernoulli effect. This decrease in air pressure causes an increase in the influx of outside air, which in turn causes the air stream to move faster. The net effect is that the average air velocity steadily increases as the center of the jet stream is approached.

150 M.P.H.

50 M.P.H.

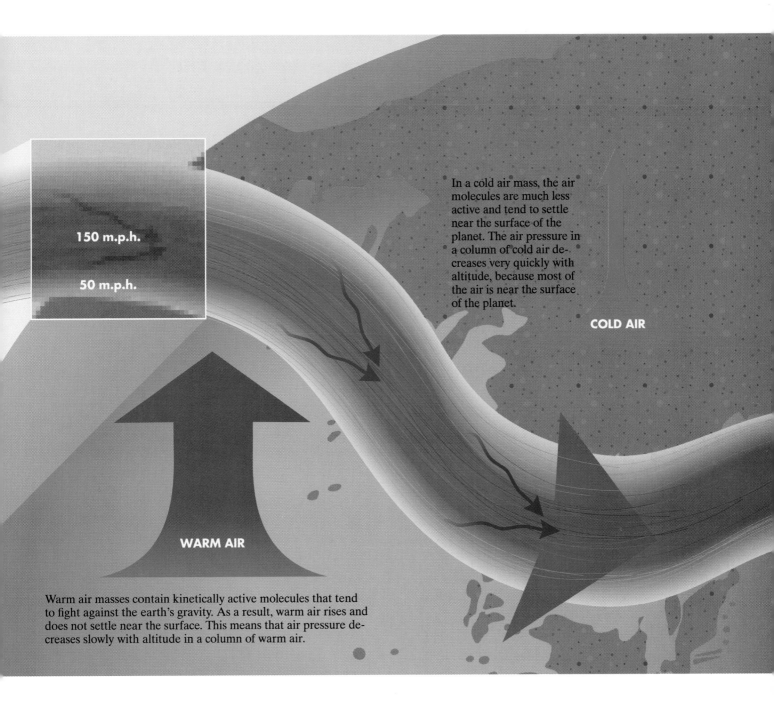

150 m.p.h.

50 m.p.h.

In a cold air mass, the air molecules are much less active and tend to settle near the surface of the planet. The air pressure in a column of cold air decreases very quickly with altitude, because most of the air is near the surface of the planet.

COLD AIR

WARM AIR

Warm air masses contain kinetically active molecules that tend to fight against the earth's gravity. As a result, warm air rises and does not settle near the surface. This means that air pressure decreases slowly with altitude in a column of warm air.

CHAPTER

8

A Current Global Model?

THE WORD *MODEL* has various meanings in the scientific realm. Some of the time, it is used as a label for a physical replica of an event or a structure; an engineer's model of a suspension bridge would be one example. Other definitions of a model are more abstract. A *numerical model* pertains to a set of equations or collected data that describes an event or a structure. An example of a numerical model would be the set of equations that govern planetary motion. The concept of being able to predict the outcome of future events based on existing data and historical trends in that data is called a forecasting model. Predicting the path of a thunderstorm or the electrical load for a power plant would be examples of forecasting models.

With more and more regularity, economists, researchers, and physical scientists are relying on a technique known as computer modeling. The advent of cheap, high-speed computational engines over the past few decades has allowed researchers to combine physical replicas, numerical models, and forecasting models into a complex amalgam of processes executed by a computer. Computer modeling has allowed humankind to embark on explorations into a physical world that was only theorized before the last half of this century. A British meteorologist, Lewis F. Richardson, became the first person to produce a guideline for a numerical model of weather forecasting during the First World War. Although he was able to produce the equations and data required to perform the calculations on which the model was dependent, Richardson estimated it would take over 60,000 people to perform the necessary calculations in a reasonable amount of time for the forecast to be useful. Today, forecasts can be performed in hours or days on a computer, depending on the complexity of the model.

Do all of these high-speed machines make the model correct? Of course not. A computer model is merely an inexpensive way to produce a complex result. The conclusions drawn from the model are only as accurate as the data and the computations fed into it by the humans running the show. Many times, the model bears out its results. For instance, a branch of computer modeling called computational fluid dynamics does, indeed, seem to produce the correct model for air passing over the wing of an aircraft, even though the calculations are amazingly complex. Airflow over a wing, however, is a model that can be verified by direct experimental evidence. Other computer driven models, such as the formation of a galaxy or the effect of carbon dioxide input on the atmosphere, are less easy to verify because they are not easily evidenced. Conducting an experiment to verify the model in these cases is either impractical or impossible because of scales of time and distance.

This book attempts to gather pieces of information and theory, from the formation of the planet through observations of our atmosphere, in order to produce a coherent model of the workings of planet Earth's current global weather situation. Whether or not this model is correct depends on the theories on which it is based.

Some of the theories making up the model are borne out by direct experimentation. Increasing the temperature in a gas, for instance, does increase the gas pressure. However, the position of the jet stream is directly verifiable by satellite imagery and penetration by aircraft, but is its formation and development as easily verified? The mechanisms involved are simple ones and are easily checked, but the sheer scale of the jet stream makes it impossible to model in any fashion other than by a computer.

Even some of the more esoteric aspects of the global model presented in these pages may be verifiable by comparative science. Recent improvements in observational astronomy, for instance, are showing us images of what we believe to be planets forming via accretion disks around other stars. If it happens elsewhere, isn't it reasonable to assume that it has happened here? Perhaps, but observe that once again, we run up against the scale of time: All of the images of possible accretion disks observed around other stars may or may not be producing planets; only another 50 million years of observations will reveal the truth.

So, keeping in mind that science is largely based on the faith that the universe observes the same rules across scales of size and time, we will return once more to our global model.

Over 4.5 billion years in our past, a new star was born out of interstellar dust and debris. The result of eons of development was the creation of a small, rocky body positioned somewhere around 90 million miles from this central star. Over a 200 million-year-long process, gases leaked out of the material in the rocky body and formed an envelope around it. Due to the size of the star and the relative positioning of this rocky body, it happened to fall into a region with a temperature range that allowed the existence of all three states of water, a molecule formed by the combination of hydrogen and oxygen.

Over the course of the existence of this rocky body, or *planet*, life evolved from the chemical soup, both thriving and adapting to the atmosphere as well as affecting the constituents of the atmosphere itself. With an increase of carbon dioxide in the atmosphere and a fixed positioning of the planet's orbit and axial stability, the global temperature began to stabilize to within a certain tolerance range of about −90° F to 120° F.

This temperature range had the advantage of allowing life to obtain a toehold while providing enough temperature variability around the globe to begin global air circulation patterns. This temperature was variable not only over latitudinal positions on the surface, but also at one spot on the surface over time. The elliptical orbit of the planet with the star at one focus, combined with the near 23° tilt of the planet's rotational axis, ensures that all points over the surface of the planet experience different amounts of solar radiation at different points in the orbit.

As different surface areas of the planet are exposed to different amounts of solar radiation, air pressure inequalities occur around the globe. The atmosphere can now be classified in terms of several large bodies, called air masses, at any given point in time. Air flow between these air masses is governed both by the temperature of the regional air mass and the rotation of the earth. Between the boundaries of some of the larger air masses, fast moving streams of air are formed. These *jet streams* are responsible for the creation and movement of large areas of clear weather and large storm systems.

Four and a half billion years after it began, Earth is a dynamic, living machine with a volatile atmosphere capable of producing and sustaining the only life in the universe of which we are currently aware. All human experience, and most certainly all human history, are a mere blink of an eye compared to the geological time scales on which the life of our planet is based.

Current Global Weather Model

By combining the elements from the various theories and observations of Earth's weather, meteorologists are able to theorize a complete global weather model that accounts for most of what humans experience in their day-to-day weather.

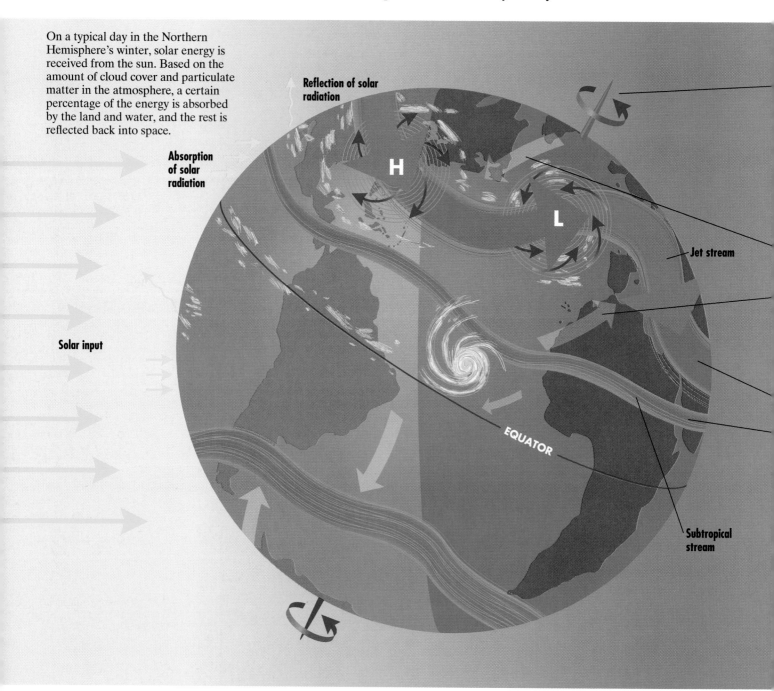

On a typical day in the Northern Hemisphere's winter, solar energy is received from the sun. Based on the amount of cloud cover and particulate matter in the atmosphere, a certain percentage of the energy is absorbed by the land and water, and the rest is reflected back into space.

Reflection of solar radiation

Absorption of solar radiation

H

L

Jet stream

Solar input

EQUATOR

Subtropical stream

The rotation of the earth induces a strange effect on moving particles called the Coriolis effect. Sometimes erroneously called a "force," this effect causes moving particles in the Northern Hemisphere to tend toward the right, and moving particles in the Southern Hemisphere to tend toward the left. It is the Coriolis effect that causes winds to blow latitudinally across the globe, rather than longitudinally as they would if the earth were not rotating.

The temperature differentials between the cold air masses in the upper latitudes and the warm air masses in the equatorial latitudes cause an air pressure imbalance, which begins a flow of air that helps to distribute heat around the globe.

Where this pressure imbalance is particularly strong, enormous rivers of air develop at high altitudes. These jet streams help create and maintain dynamic weather systems that move across the face of the planet. Although the jet stream–induced highs and lows are at times unpredictable, the rule of thumb is that high-pressure cells are formed as the air descends into a trough in the stream, and low-pressure cells form as the air ascends back to a ridge.

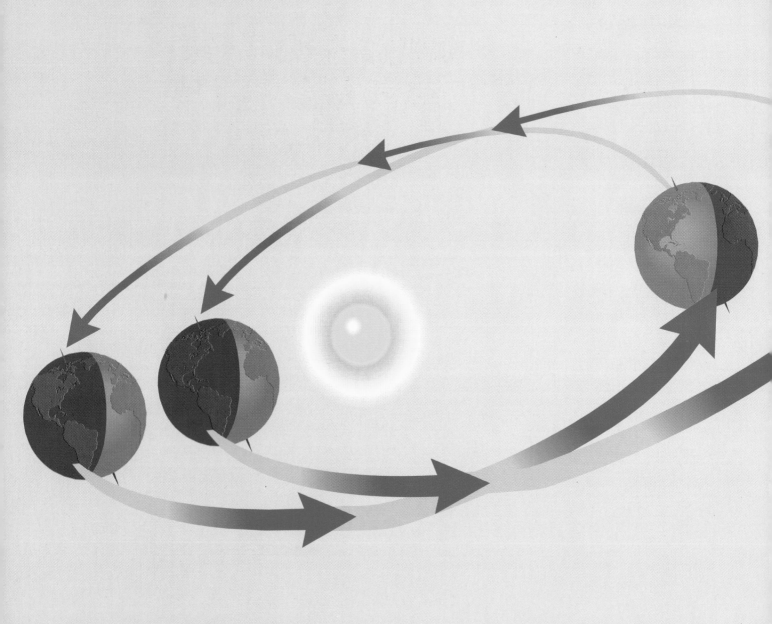

MILD WEATHER: EARTH AND ITS SEASONS

CONTENTS

OVERVIEW

METEOROLOGISTS TEND TO classify wind motions into one of four categories of scale: *Planetary scale motions* are the largest scale at which wind motion occurs. Planetary scale winds usually are on par with those of continents and oceans. *Synoptic scale motions,* although large, are smaller than planetary scale winds. Synoptic scale winds tend to measure several hundreds of miles. *Mesoscale motions* are on the order of ten to a few hundred miles in size. *Small scale motions* are essentially everything else. Small scale motions are often less than a few miles in size.

The previous part of this book referred to wind motions on a planetary scale: the jet streams and air mass motions. This section also talks about wind motions on a planetary scale: the distribution of air and temperature throughout the globe on a yearly cycle. The residents of Earth commonly refer to this phenomenon as seasonal variation, or simply, the seasons.

There are other scales to take into account besides scales of size, for example, scales of time. There is more to the cyclic timings of Earth than humans can perceive with their five senses. Recall that Earth is a *dynamic* weather machine and that it is in a constant state of flux. Humans experience Earth's cyclic changes as orderly changes in the temperature throughout the year: It is colder in the winter months than it is in the summer, for instance. However, some of Earth's cycles occur on time scales that are beyond human experience.

Earth has gone through myriad changes in its existence, but certain long-term patterns seem to persist throughout its history. The planet has a habit, for instance, of flipping its magnetic poles every 25,000 years or so: magnetic north suddenly becomes magnetic south. In addition, the planet's atmosphere seems to go through a natural, cyclic dip in its temperature range, called an ice age, with remarkable regularity.

Although long timescale changes do occur, humankind is not likely to experience them at any point in its near future. Nonetheless, these long-term variations do seem to have happened, and they may have had profound effects on today's weather situation.

All things change, and that, perhaps, is as it should be.

Cycles and the Seasons

THE UNIVERSE IS constantly changing. Galaxies evolve and caterpillars metamorphose into butterflies. All of these transformations from one state to another require energy, and recall that there is no such thing as perpetual motion: Energy taken from a source deprives that source of the equivalent amount of energy. Obviously, the process of energy transfer could not possibly continue forever, since the universe is of finite size and, therefore, has a finite amount of energy. Although the previous statement implies that the universe will eventually run out of steam, the process of energy redistribution can perpetuate the course of state changes over a long period of time.

Energy redistribution is another way of thinking of the cycles of nature. For a moment, consider a single wheat plant. If this plant were to grow, drop its seeds, and then be removed from the soil, it would take only a few planting periods before the soil was depleted of organic material to nurture plants; wheat would cease to grow in that environment. On the other hand, if the wheat plant were allowed to grow, drop its seeds, and then die in the soil, it would begin a process called decomposition, a breakdown of its chemical bonds. The soil would regain much of the organic material that it gave up to the plant, and the useful growing period of the soil would be greatly extended.

Now consider cyclic events on a larger scale. The astronomical seasons of Earth are due to a combination of the tilt of the axis of the planet and the journey of the planet around its star, the sun. This orbital process has been in motion for well over 4 billion years and will likely continue at least that far into the future. The cycle in this case is the orbital period of the planet.

Earth and all of the planets are in a constant "fall" towards the sun. Although this process will continue for an extremely long time, it will eventually take its toll on the Earth-Sun system. Earth, in continuing its endless drop towards a gravitational minimum, is imparting its kinetic energy to the sun. If other processes do not interfere, Earth will eventually transfer so much of its orbital energy to the sun that its orbital velocity will decrease to the point where it no longer can balance the gravitational pull of the sun with forward velocity: Earth's orbit will decay.

The orbit of Earth around the sun produces four distinct seasonal variations on the surface of the earth. In the Northern Hemisphere, December 21 is the start of winter and June 21 is the start of summer. Consider for a moment what is implied by this concept. June 21 is the astronomical beginning of summer in the Northern Hemisphere, which means that on June 21, the Northern Hemisphere sees the sun reach its zenith, or highest point, in its track across the sky. At this point, the Northern Hemisphere is experiencing its greatest influx of solar radiation. Yet, most denizens of the Northern Hemisphere will be the first to proclaim that the hottest days of the summer are near the end of July to the beginning of August. (Even these reports vary depending on the latitude of the observer.) Why does this happen?

Approximately 50% of the solar radiation that reaches the earth is absorbed by either surface rock or surface water. This short-wave high-energy radiation is slowly reradiated back as a long-wave infrared radiation, or heat energy. By this process of energy absorption, the Northern Hemisphere begins to assimilate quite a bit of solar radiation, culminating at its peak on June 21. The total amount of heat energy trapped in the earth, atmosphere, and ocean is called a *heat budget* or *energy budget*.

Although the amount of solar input begins to decline after this date, the input from the sun is assisted by input from reradiation of stored solar heat. This effect, called *heat lag*, is also referred to as having a *positive heat budget*. The result is that the hottest days of the summer occur weeks or months after the astronomical beginning of summer. Heat lag also accounts for the coldest part of the winter occurring long after December 21 in the Northern Hemisphere. It is also responsible for the hottest part of the day occurring a few hours after the sun reaches its daily zenith at noon.

Because of heat lag, there was a need for meteorologists to break seasonal definitions into two categories: astronomical and meteorologic seasons.

Astronomical seasons are the quarterly divisions that define where Earth is in its orbit with respect to the sun. These are the seasonal dates that are taught to us very early in life. Because these periods are easily defined by measurable effects (the sun reaching its zenith, for instance), these seasonal dates have been noted in one form or another throughout recorded history. Most agricultural societies, for example, recognize the summer and winter solstices and celebrate them as seasonal passings. *Meteorologic seasons* are seasonal definitions defined by the less strict concept of local temperature deviations. The high point of summer is not necessarily June 21, but rather when the days have become the hottest. Likewise, the phrase *the middle of winter* applies to a region when it is at its coldest, which is not necessarily the period around December 21.

What defines a meteorologic season is quite a bit more vague than the textbook-strict astronomical definitions. Heat is absorbed and reemitted by water much more slowly than by land, so it is not uncommon for coastal areas to feel the effects of winter later into the astronomical season than do inland areas. Many areas in the lower latitudes never experience a period where the temperature drops below freezing, and, as such, the inhabitants of these areas never feel winter.

Temperature Differentials in the Northern Hemisphere Caused by Heat Lag

Vernal Equinox

As the temperature increases due to an influx of solar radiant energy, the energy absorbed by the earth increases. When the amount of solar radiant energy begins to decrease, energy stored in the earth's surface rocks and water reradiate back into the infrared to help keep the temperature high.

RELATIVE TEMPERATURE

J   F   M   A

If the earth were a perfect reflector of solar radiant energy, its temperature curve would follow the yellow line. The temperature would peak in the Northern Hemisphere on June 21 and would reach a minimum on December 21. This line represents the temperature expected due to the astronomical seasons.

The shaded area represents the temperature differential between the expected temperature due to incoming solar radiation and the actual temperature due to reradiated heat energy. For the Northern Hemisphere, the temperature differential causes the average temperature to lag behind the incoming temperature prior to midyear. In other words, the land, soil, lakes, and oceans have given back much of their heat energy and are busy absorbing new, incoming energy faster than they are reradiating it. The situation is reversed in the last half of the year; the earth's surface has been saturated with incoming energy and reradiates more than it takes in. The result is warmer temperatures than would be expected, given the position of Earth in its orbit.

The earth absorbs nearly 50% of the incoming energy from the sun. This energy is absorbed in the short-wave high-energy end of the spectrum, and reradiated as long-wave low-energy infrared radiation which, in turn, is reabsorbed by the atmosphere. The average Northern Hemisphere temperature is, therefore, represented by the purple temperature line. This line represents the actual temperature that constitutes the meteorologic seasons.

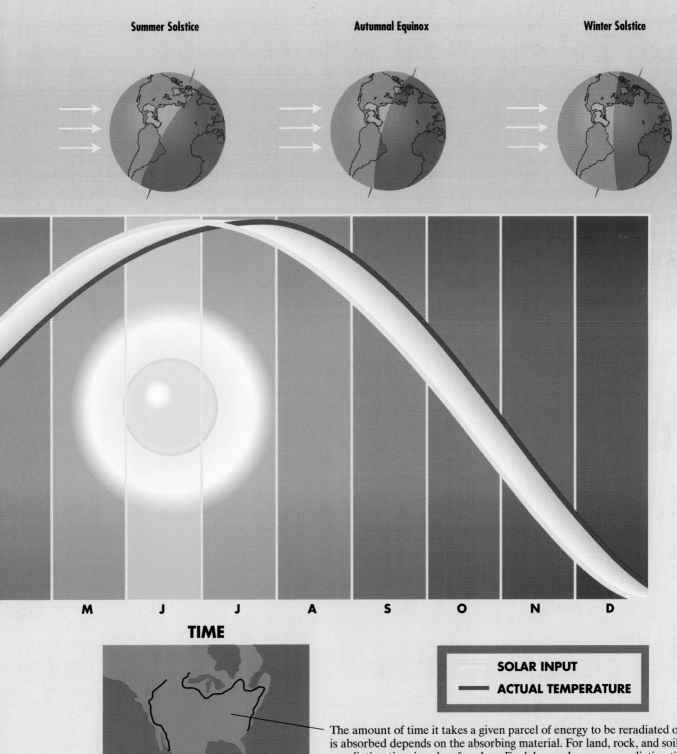

Summer Solstice   Autumnal Equinox   Winter Solstice

M M J J A S O N D

TIME

SOLAR INPUT

ACTUAL TEMPERATURE

The amount of time it takes a given parcel of energy to be reradiated once it is absorbed depends on the absorbing material. For land, rock, and soil, the reradiation time is only a few days. For lakes and oceans, reradiation time is on the order of weeks. Using North America as an example, the areas around the coastal regions are cooler than the inland regions during the summer months and warmer than the inland regions during the winter months.

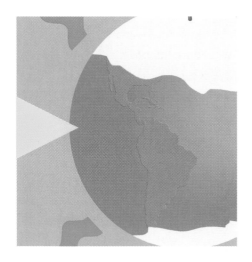

CHAPTER
10

Cycles: A Larger
Climatological Picture

SEASONAL CHANGES IN the global temperature are part of a cycle of climatic events that is well behaved, well understood and very predictable. The yearly climatic cycles of the seasons have a relatively short period—well within the lifetime of a single human being. When we expand our horizons toward a larger time frame, an amazing picture begins to emerge. It becomes evident that our four-season-a-year cycles of climatic change are actually ripples on a larger wave.

Paleoclimatologists use more than trapped air bubbles to measure the weather of the past. Other tools of this science include drilling several hundred meters into Earth's crust for thermal measurements trapped in the mantle, as well as examining indirect evidence, such as tree growth rings, historical records, and archeological findings.

To be sure, some of this evidence is prone to misinterpretation: Historical records prior to the late nineteenth century can be anecdotal; tree growth can be retarded for reasons other than the weather; and borehole drilling is concentrated mostly in the northern latitude regions, so it doesn't give us a clear picture of the entire planet. In addition, the farther that paleoclimatologists look back in time, the more difficult it is to gather information. Obtaining data from prehistoric times requires some clever data collection techniques and a lot of luck. However, by piecing together the evidence obtained from the constant probing into our past, paleoclimatologists have assembled a million-year-old story of long-term climatic cycles; but it is a story currently devoid of an ending.

From the paleoclimatological records, it is clear that in the past 1 million years, the earth has been through ten ice ages, during which the global temperature dropped to a point where significant climatological changes took place. The current average yearly global temperature on planet Earth is computed by averaging temperatures through all of the four seasons from pole to pole. The result is a temperature averaging about 15.5°C, or 60° F, which is quite warm if you examine the temperature chart over the past million years.

A change in the global average by even a few degrees would have a profound impact on regional surface air temperatures. The last ice age, which occurred approximately 18,000 years ago, was at the tail end of a period in the earth's geologic time scale called the Pleistocene. The result of that ice age was that the global average temperature decreased by approximately 5° C, or 9° F.

This translated to a range of temperature drops from 20° C (36° F) in the polar regions to only a couple of degrees in the equatorial regions.

The effect of this kind of temperature change is apparent when comparisons are made between the last portion of the Pleistocene and the *Holocene*, which is our current geologic age. During the last ice age, that 5° C change resulted in a *cryosphere*, the sum total of all of the earth's ice mass, which was over twice as large as it is today. This increase in the ice packs resulted in a global sea-level drop on the order of 100 meters. Glaciers, massive frozen rivers of flowing ice, extended through most of North America and Northern Europe carving out many of the current lakes and valleys of those regions. The glaciers deposited rocks from the arctic regions as far south as Wisconsin and France. Data obtained from Antarctica confirm that the effects of this temperature drop were apparent on a global scale.

The earth's climate began to grow warmer about 15,000 years ago, and the earth was considered officially out of its last ice age approximately 10,000 years ago. The temperatures increased, the glaciers retreated, and the sea levels rose. Although the climate change was gradual, it was faster than biological adaptations would allow for, and mass extinctions occurred at all levels. The earth saw the end of animals such as the mastodon, the woolly mammoth, and several species of saber-toothed carnivores.

The Pleistocene ice age is the temperature-drop period that is studied the most by paleoclimatologists, because it occurred the most recently. It is important to remember, however, that the cycle of temperature drops occurred at least nine other times over the course of a 1-million-year time frame. During each period of temperature drop, evidence of massive global climatological change exists.

What does all this mean? Why do these global temperature drops occur, and are we going to experience any more within the scope of human existence? No one knows for certain.

There are two main schools of thought as to why ice ages occur. The first is that cyclic global temperature fluctuations are due to influences external to the earth-atmosphere-ocean-cryosphere system. There are a number of candidates for these external influences, ranging from periodic fluctuations in the orbit of Earth to cyclic fluctuations in the energy output of the sun. Could any of these external influences be responsible? The debate has been raging for over 50 years. A Serbian paleoclimatic researcher named Milutin Milankovitch proposed in 1941 that periodic vacillations in Earth's orbit can easily cause large-scale swings in global temperature, with ice ages most likely to occur when solar radiation is decreased over the Northern Hemisphere.

Other climatologists and meteorologists feel that the majority of the external influences would be too weak to account for all of the ice ages.

However, one powerful external influence may have a role in these periodic temperature swings. Astronomers have coined the term *albedo* to refer to the fraction of radiant energy reflected by a body. A planetary body may reflect energy from the cloud tops, ice packs, snow, oceans, or vegetation. The albedo range runs from 0 (complete absorption of all incoming energy) to 1 (complete reflection of all incoming energy). The global albedo average for Earth, for instance, is 0.31. By way of comparison, the global albedo for the planet Venus is 0.63, and the global albedo for the planet Mercury is 0.05.

If the incoming solar radiation to the earth were decreased for an extended period of time, the total size of the cryosphere would increase. Ice is an excellent reflectant of radiant energy, so the overall albedo of the earth would increase. This increase in the albedo would mean that the amount of solar radiation absorbed by the surface of the planet would decrease, allowing for the further expansion of the cryosphere, which would further increase the albedo. This feedback mechanism could be self-sustaining for a short time until the solar radiation increased sufficiently to overcome the effect of an increased albedo.

The second school of thought is that the source of the temperature periodicity lies within the earth-atmosphere-ocean-cryosphere system itself. Given the current range of solar energy input, it is possible to conceive of two or more naturally occurring states of the earth-atmosphere-ocean-cryosphere system that would produce the same energy balance numbers. (Recall that the *energy balance* is the numeric juggling of the total energy input against the total energy output to produce a stable energy system.) In simpler terms, these periodic fluctuations in the earth's temperature occur because it is natural for these states to exist.

We have seen that on a very short-term scale, over the period of a year, the regional temperatures oscillate to produce seasons. On a very long-term scale, a scale that includes a million years of geologic time, the global temperature also oscillates. The debate still rages about why exactly this periodicity occurs, but there is very little doubt in researchers' minds that it does occur. Now, let us focus our time scale to a period of a few hundred thousand years and examine the temperature cycles we find there.

As the earth was retreating from the Pleistocene Ice Age and the global temperature was on the increase, there was a sudden decrease in temperatures in the North Atlantic and Southern Hemisphere regions. This specific midrange temperature fluctuation is referred to as the Younger Dryas. The temperature decrease in this period lasted for only 500 to 700 years, and is thought to be attributed to changes in the Atlantic ocean circulation patterns.

Younger Dryas is a special case, not because these midscale temperature decreases have not occurred throughout history, but because it occurred recently enough for evidence to have been preserved and recovered. It is far easier to gather evidence from a 10,000-year ice age 800,000 years in the past then it is to gather evidence from a much smaller temperature perturbation lasting only 500 years, 10,000 years ago.

There is evidence from recent historical times that these midscale cycles are still occurring, although this evidence is not globally consistent, as it was not reported by all civilizations. However, there is significant evidence that during the 300 years from 1550 to 1850, the global temperature of the earth dipped significantly. The world's glaciers advanced through the Northern Hemisphere, and middle-latitude regions in the Northern and Southern Hemisphere had particularly harsh winters. This dip in the global temperature scales is commonly referred to as the Little Ice Age.

Long-, Mid- and Short-term Global Temperature Cycles

1,000,000 YEARS TO PRESENT

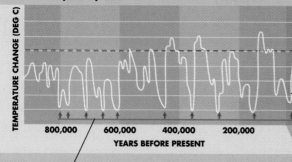

Current global temperature average

The last ice age occurred at the end of the geologic era known as the Pleistocene. It began about 20,000 years ago, and by all accounts began tapering off about 15,000 years ago. By 10,000 years ago, the last of the ice ages had passed, leaving in its wake reformed landscapes, new lakes, seas, and rivers, and the extinction of several hundred species of animal life.

Paleoclimatological evidence suggests that there have been a total of ten ice ages, or significant temperature drops, over the course of the past 1 million years. These ice ages lower the global temperature average almost 5° C (9° F), resulting in increased glacial activity, lower sea levels, and an increase in the earth's ice mass, or cryosphere. Ice ages usually last about 10,000 years.

10,000 YEARS TO PRESENT

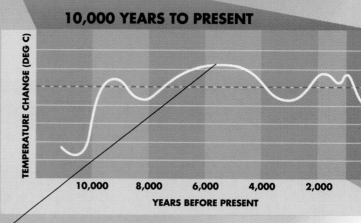

The geologic age from the end of the Pleistocene (10,000 years ago) to the present day is called the Holocene era. Approximately 6,000 years ago, the global temperature reached a maximum of about 1.5° C (2.7° F) hotter than the global average temperature today. This temperature maximum ended abruptly as the surface temperature of the planet entered a period of cooling.

Over the course of the last 1 million years, paleoclimatology has revealed that Earth's global temperature has not remained constant. Periodic fluctuations occur regardless of the time scale used for examination.

Current global temperature average

There is evidence in our past that small-scale temperature fluctuations (those lasting about a few hundred years) occur with some cyclic regularity. Often these small-scale fluctuations occur when the planet is emerging from an ice age, possibly because the planet is attempting to regulate its temperature. The last known global temperature drop, however, seems to have occurred from the years 1550 to 1850. This 300-year period is referred to as the Little Ice Age.

Reducing our scale still further, we can observe the local short-term temperature cycles that are apparent at any point on the temperature graph. Closer to home, the earth seems to have gone through a complete, nearly sinusoidal oscillation, or regular period fluctuation, of temperature with a period of about 1,000 years. The warmer-than-average period from AD 1000 to AD 1400 is referred to as the Medieval Warm Period, and the colder-than-average period from 1550 to 1850 is the Little Ice Age. While examining this graph, keep in mind that if we were to break the time scale down further, the yearly periodic four-season temperature oscillations would become visible.

1,000 YEARS TO PRESENT

TEMPERATURE CHANGE (DEG C)

Current global temperature average

1000 AD   1500 AD   1900 AD

What Causes Ice Ages?

All we know is that periodically, the earth's global average temperature oscillates irregularly both on a long-term and short-term time scale. But what
causes the temperature variations? No one really knows, though a lot of theories and ideas—both realistic and fantastic—are being talked about.

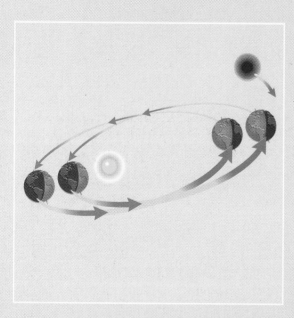

**Current position of
Earth's spin axis**

**Past or future
position of spin
axis due to
precession**

23.5°

?

**How great is the
difference? No
one is certain.**

In 1941, it was first proposed that the orbit of Earth
vacillates, or wavers, at irregular intervals. If they
exist, what causes these vacillations? Perhaps they
are a normal part of Earth's orbit, a memento from
the time of its creation. Perhaps a large, massive
body such as another star occasionally passes close
to our solar system and tugs on the orbits of all the
planets. Perhaps the orbital vacillations do not occur
at all.

The axis of Earth may wobble, like a spinning top. If
it exists, what causes this wobble? It is known that
Earth's rotational axis regularly *precesses*, or slowly
moves in a circle about the spin axis, which is an
imaginary line through Earth and perpendicular to
the plane of Earth's orbit. (That is why the North
Star, Polaris, is no longer north—although it was a
few thousand years ago.) Perhaps the precession of
the axis is indicative of other, unknown motions in
Earth's axis.

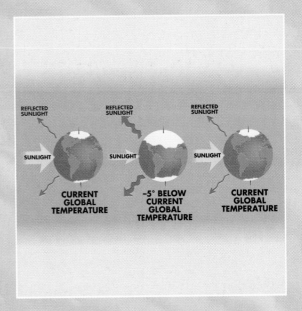

It is known that the earth goes through periods of large scale volcanic activity. It is conceivable that during these periods, enormous amounts of volcanic debris are thrown up into the tropopause in sufficient quantity to diminish the incoming radiant energy from the sun for long periods of time. This is not as farfetched as it sounds. It is suspected that the eruption in 1883 of the West Indonesian volcano Krakatoa, which spread debris as far as Madagascar and generated many tsunami, was responsible for an abnormally cold summer that year.

If the input of solar energy were to decrease for a long enough period, because of either a decrease of energy output from the sun or a blockage of sunlight by debris in the upper atmosphere, the cryosphere, or total ice mass of planet Earth, may increase. If this were to happen, the amount of reflected sunlight would increase, and the amount of energy absorbed by the earth and oceans would decrease. This would further lower the global temperature and increase the size of the cryosphere. This feedback mechanism might be self-sustaining until the solar energy increased in sufficient quantity to reduce the size of the cryosphere. Ice in this condition would take a long time to retreat, allowing for the 10,000-year length of the ice ages.

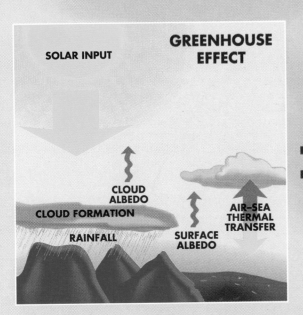

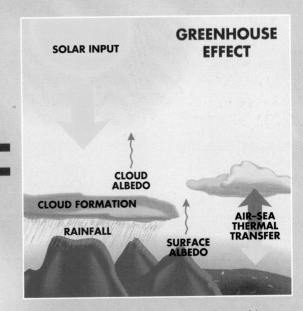

Another camp in the ice age question claims that, due to the range of solar energy raining down on the earth, the earth's energy budget (the balancing of energy input with energy storage and energy output) can exist over a vast range of conditions. In other words, temperature fluctuations over a very long time scale occur because it is perfectly natural for them to exist.

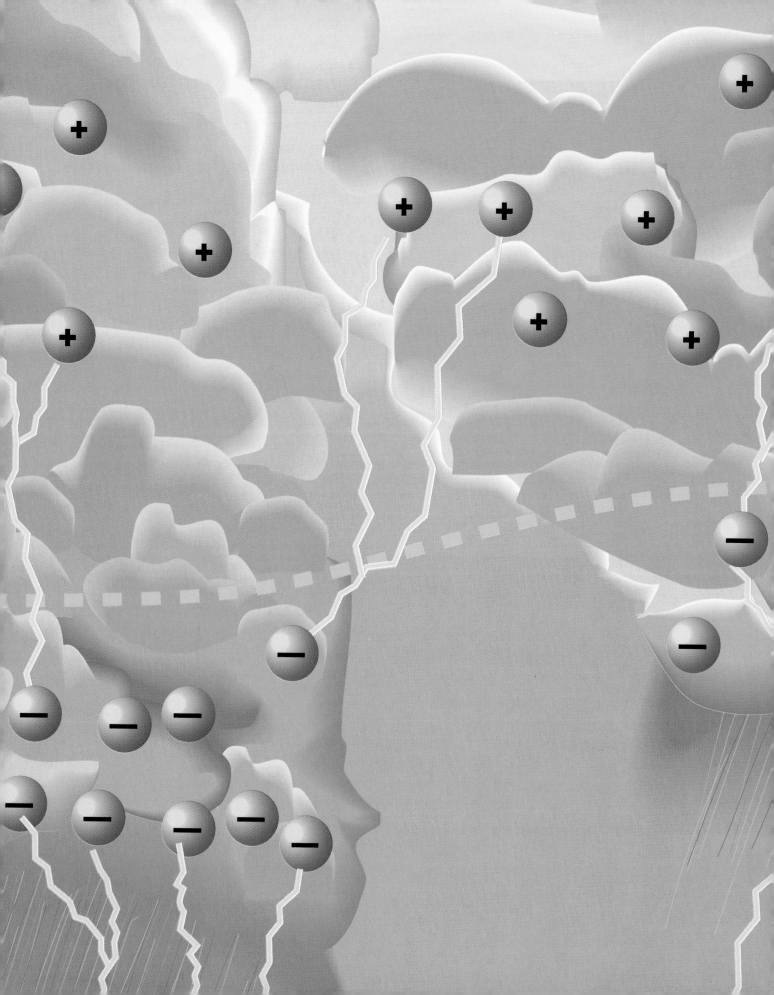

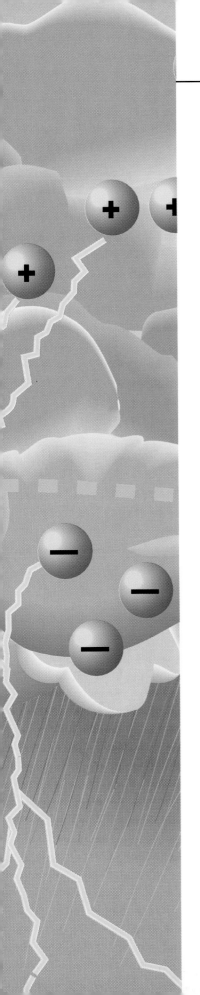

TANTRUMS: VIOLENT WEATHER

CONTENTS

THE ATMOSPHERIC MASS of Earth, when taken on the whole, is largely *adiabatic*—the atmosphere does not gain or lose heat energy, as the net energy fluctuation is approximately zero. On a planetary scale, Earth's atmosphere is remarkably self-regulatory, so it makes sense that its overall response to environmental changes are benign and cyclical.

When you shrink the scales of size and time, however, the atmosphere of Earth seems anything but benign. Over any given week at nearly any point on the globe, an observer on the ground will see meteorologic changes ranging from clear, cloudless skies to raging thunderstorms, blizzards, or worse. These extrovert activities of the atmosphere are referred to by meteorologists and laypeople alike as storms. Loosely defined, a *storm* is any atmospheric disturbance in an area's normal weather patterns. In a more day-to-day sense, storms are also associated with violent, or at least unpleasant, consequences such as damaging winds or relentless precipitation.

For millennia, the occurrence patterns of storms and storm systems seemed beyond the reach of human understanding. The sudden, almost emotional outbursts of violent weather puzzled, frightened, and disturbed human beings through recorded history, and more than likely even before records were kept. Anthropomorphic reasoning was applied to explain these weather patterns; certainly only the navigation of some unseen, conscious entity could explain why on a calm, summer day, a sudden raging thunderstorm appears. Only an emotional being would send enormous winds careening through a village or farmland with reckless abandon, killing anything caught in their path.

At any given moment, somewhere on the globe a thunderstorm is occurring, a typhoon is raging, or a blizzard is blowing. Current estimates are that there are approximately 100 cloud-to-ground lightning strikes on our planet every second. Each year, tens of thousands of people lose their homes to a raging storm, and thousands more die because of weather-related activity. For a weather machine that has been painted as calm, slow to change, and largely cyclical in its temperature variations, these seem like alarming statistics. Even in this age of global satellite coverage, sophisticated computer modeling, and five-day weather forecasts, it is not uncommon to be caught completely off-guard by an approaching thunderstorm, tornado, or hurricane. Why? What is it in our global weather environment that causes these tantrums?

The universe is very large and complex, and the planet Earth is part of that complexity. Local variations and fluctuations in the air currents and global weather condition are required for the atmosphere to continue to function as a life-protecting environment.

The local storm systems and tantrums that our atmosphere concocts are not brought about because something has gone wrong with the system, but rather occur naturally because things are working correctly. For instance, the 100 lightning flashes occur each second because the planet Earth wants to maintain a negative electrical polarity; the lightning is a way of changing the polarity of pockets of positive charge that form near thunderstorms.

Put into other terms, storms—and all their consequences—are simply the cost of doing business on planet Earth.

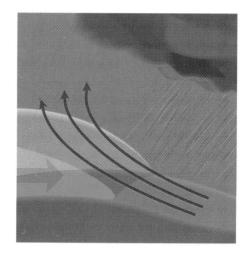

Lines of the Storm

THE WEATHER EVENTS that we refer to as storm systems are generated in a variety of ways and sizes. They can either be extremely local, such as a tornado, or occur as synoptic scale events such as hurricanes or mesoscale events such as a line of thunderstorms. To discuss all of these events in detail would require another book, and looking through a college meteorology section of a university bookstore will reveal several on the topic. The one element that all of these events have in common, however, is that they are generated by interactions between regions of different temperature and, therefore, pressure (processes that the reader will be familiar with at this point).

A moving mass of warm, moist air encounters a cold air mass and climbs above it where the moisture condenses out, forming clouds. This is the concept of dynamic lifting as applied to cloud formation. The same principle is applied in the construction of a *front*, or boundary, between a warm air mass and a cold air mass. Once again, the sun comes into play, creating a temperature differential between two regions that will affect the temperature of the air masses above these regions. Either a high- or low-pressure system will begin the motion of one or more of these air masses, and eventually two air masses of different temperatures will come in contact with each other. The boundary, or *interface*, between these two interacting air masses is where the action begins.

Cold air masses are extremely dense when compared with warmer air. Because there is less kinetic energy in the air molecules of the cold air mass, gravity tends to cause the cold air to hug the ground, which accounts for the mass's density. To imagine a cold air mass on the move, think of pouring a thick, viscous material—such as syrup—onto a tabletop. The syrup tends to cling to the surface of the table, spreading out evenly in all directions. The edge of the syrup tends to have a steep slope, lending a bluntness to the boundary of the syrup mass.

A cold air mass behaves in a manner similar to the syrup, and when it encounters a lighter, less dense mass of warm air, its tendency is to shove underneath the warmer air. The front formed by such an interaction is called a cold front, and it is a key player in the formation of much storm activity. As the cold air mass moves under the warm air mass, the momentum of the colder air forces the warmer air up. If the warm air mass is moisture laden, clouds will form due to dynamic lifting. Because of the bluntness of the edge of a cold front, observers on the ground may experience a drastic shift from warm to cold air as the front passes over them.

The reverse of the above situation can occur if the cold air mass is stationary and a moving warmer mass of air enters the region. In this scenario, the warmer air mass encounters the stationary cold air with less momentum due to the lower density of the warm air mass. The warm air mass gently slides over the cold air mass obstacle, forming clouds and storm systems as it rises. As it advances, the warm air mass slowly "erodes" the colder air. This type of front, a *warm front*, can also result in inclement weather.

A warm front's leading edge is not blunt as that of a cold front. Because the moving warm air mass has less momentum, it has a harder time forcing its way into the cold air mass region. The result is a frontal boundary that gradually slopes upward, sometimes taking a hundred miles or so to rise to the dew point altitude. To an observer on the ground, the change in weather takes place gradually as the front moves into the region.

Both of these frontal systems can and do cause large, advancing lines of storm systems that gradually move across a given region. The energy supplied to these storms is supplemented by the actions of the advancing front itself. The moving air masses involved in the storm fronts have momentum, which contribute to a storm's kinetic energy.

Evaporation of water takes heat energy, so when water evaporates, or becomes water vapor, the water molecules trap a certain amount of that heat energy. This trapped energy is referred to as latent heat. As water vapor is transported to the condensation level along a frontal line, the latent heat is released during the condensation process. This energy input also contributes to an existing frontal storm's energy system. Finally, once a storm begins, it perpetuates the process of thermal energy transfer by creating localized pressure differences that cause warm and cold air to mix. A greater temperature imbalance results, which, in turn, adds to the energy input of the storm system.

If the front is long enough and the conditions are right throughout a large section of the front, several storm systems extremely close together can organize themselves into a mesoscale structure commonly referred to as a squall line. Large cumulonimbus towers arrange themselves close together along the line, giving rise to the other title for a squall line: a *line thunderstorm*. Squall lines are common in middle latitude regions, including the United States, during the summer months.

One of the striking features of a squall line is the front boundary formed by the advancing cold downdraft air mass. This leading edge is called a *gust front* and marks the leading edge of the penetrating cold air. The gust front is similar to the larger, synoptic scale cold front. However, a gust front is always the result of a storm system—whether a storm system formed by a squall line or an isolated thunderstorm. A cold front is more commonly associated with the boundary between two larger scale air masses.

The position of a gust front relative to the storm system itself varies based on the maturity of the storm. When a storm system is newly forming, the gust front is usually just ahead of the storm's precipitation. When a storm begins to decay, however, the gust front may far outdistance the rest of the storm and appear as an isolated event. The passage of a gust front is evidenced by the sudden, dramatic change from surrounding warm air to cold, downdraft air from the storm system.

Although gust fronts are often invisible, their existence can be revealed through several different mechanisms. One of these mechanisms is the inclusion of particulate matter in the warm air mass through which the colder gust front is passing. Dust or other particles in the warm air mass ride high into the air as the gust front plows into the region. The resulting dust clouds are quite common in the southwestern and dust-bowl areas of the United States.

Another way in which gust fronts are rendered visible is through moisture in the warm air mass. As the warm, moist air rides up the leading edge of the gust front, it can hit its dew point temperature almost immediately. The result is an impressive condensation layer covering the leading edge of the front. This effect produces an *arcus cloud.* Either through particulate matter or condensation, a visible, advancing gust front is an awe-inspiring sight, both to the seasoned professional and the first-time observer.

Air Mass Interaction and the Creation of Fronts

Creation of a Cold Front

Once set in motion, the kinetic energy of a dense cold air mass gains momentum. When this moving air mass encounters a mass of lighter, less dense warm air, the cold air mass shoves its way underneath the warmer air. As the warm air rises rapidly along the blunt face of the cold air, it rapidly reaches its condensation, or dew-point, level, forming clouds. Often, these conditions lead to the formation of cumulus clouds, which can create thunderstorms along the front.

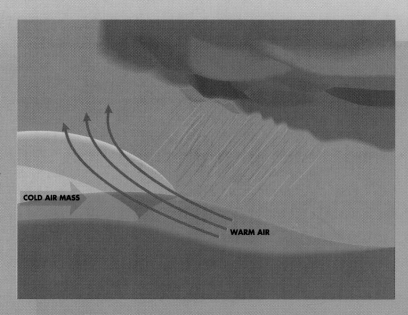

COLD AIR MASS

WARM AIR

Creation of a Warm Front

A different situation arises when a moving mass of warm air encounters a stationary mass of cold air. Although the moving warm air mass does not pick up as much momentum as an equivalent mass of colder air, it does manage to erode the cold air. In this scenario, the warm air climbs gradually on top of the colder air mass. The end result is that the warm air is once again transported to its dew-point level, where moisture condenses out, forming clouds and inclement weather.

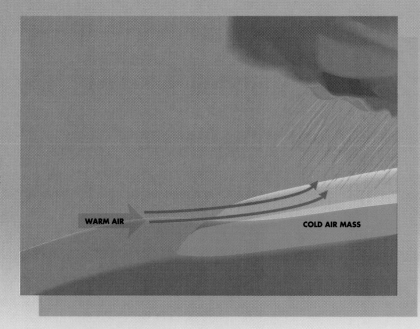

WARM AIR

COLD AIR MASS

An air mass is defined in meteorologic circles as a large body of air, often synoptic in scale, that has homogeneous properties of temperature, pressure, moisture content, and stability. Some typical air masses that may be found over North America are depicted here: cold, continental polar air moves in from the Arctic; cool, maritime Pacific air moves in from the northern Pacific; warm, maritime Pacific air moves in from the South Pacific; and hot maritime Gulf-Caribbean air moves up from the South Atlantic. The interaction of all of these air masses can cause inclement weather along their boundaries, or fronts.

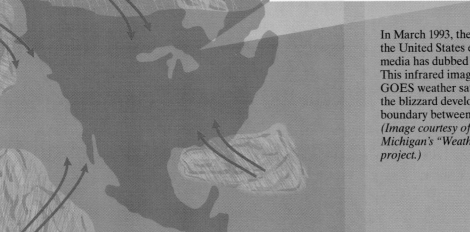

In March 1993, the eastern seaboard of the United States experienced what the media has dubbed "The Blizzard of '93." This infrared image taken from the GOES weather satellite clearly shows the blizzard developing along the boundary between two air masses. *(Image courtesy of the University of Michigan's "Weather Underground" project.)*

Anatomy of a Typical Squall Line Storm

The advancing cold, downdraft air from the squall line acts like a mini cold front and shoves its way into the warmer moist air. The warmer air gets lifted rapidly up and beyond the inversion layer, where it reaches its condensation level. To an observer, the condensation level is the first sign of the advancing storm, as it is clearly visible as a dark cloud base.

COLD AIR

56,000 FT

50,000 FT

43,800 FT

TROPOPAUSE

37,400 FT

31,000 FT

Due to strong winds at high altitudes in a squall line, the updraft air eventually gains high velocity away from the advancing squall. A cloud structure known as an anvil leads the way for the advancing gust front. An *anvil* is caused by vertical wind shear: Wind is just blowing faster at the higher elevations, causing the cloud to distend in the direction of the storm. Because of the altitude obtained by this updraft, the anvil is composed, typically, of fine-grain ice crystals at or near the tropopause level.

24,600 FT

18,200 FT

■ ■ ■ ■ ■ ■ ■ ■ ■ ■ **0° C**

12,800 FT

The intersection between the cold downdraft and the warm, moist air forms a gust front, which is roughly analogous to a cold front but on a much smaller scale. A gust front brings with it an incredible change in wind direction and velocity, called a wind shear. This is caused by the warm air moving swiftly up one side of the interface (called the updraft), and the cold air moving swiftly down the other side of the interface (called the downdraft). If the warm air contains sufficient moisture and the temperature differential between the two air masses is great enough, a cloud structure will condense out along the face of the gust front. This structure is called an arcus cloud.

A local mass of unstable air encounters the leading edge of the colder squall line. Quite often, this air mass is capped by a weak inversion layer. This cap prevents premature convection and allows the storm front to form along the squall line.

DRY AIR

INVERSION LAYER

6,400 FT

MOIST AIR

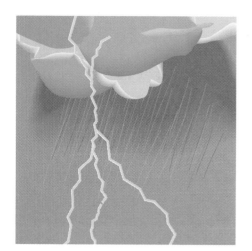

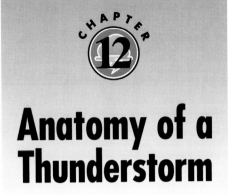

Anatomy of a Thunderstorm

THE STORMS DISCUSSED in the previous chapter were created by *frontal systems*: two air masses of vastly different temperatures colliding. If there is sufficient moisture in the warm air mass and enough momentum in the collision to transport that warm air to the condensation level, then a storm system can result.

There are other types of thunderstorms that are formed entirely from local conditions. *Air mass,* or *convective,* thunderstorms occur when energy from the sun warms an area of ground or water to a temperature sufficient to cause a parcel of air to rise. As is obvious from the formation process, air mass thunderstorms are normally only produced in the areas of the globe where the local environment is warm and wet, such as the tropics and the midtropical regions. In the summer months, however, it is quite common for thunderstorms to develop in middle-latitude regions.

In the late 1940s, air mass thunderstorms were intensely studied in a program called the Thunderstorm Project. Because of the efforts of the Thunderstorm Project, the first theories of the creation, life, and death of thunderstorms were formed. As meteorological analysis and data collection techniques improved with advancements in technology, the early theories of the Thunderstorm Project were confirmed, and more data has been added to give meteorologists a complete picture of an air mass thunderstorm. Today, the life cycle of a thunderstorm is a well-understood process.

A thunderstorm lives its life in three distinct stages: the cumulus stage, the mature stage, and the dissipation stage. Depending on local conditions of temperature and air stability, the entire life cycle can last up to an hour, although half-hour life cycles are more typical. Air outflow from the storm also varies wildly with local conditions, and severe thunderstorms can spawn tornadoes. Thunderstorms also can generate enormous electrical discharges in the form of lightning, although this process is just beginning to be understood in detail.

On a typical warm, humid summer day, the heat of the day takes its toll on the surface of the earth. The earth absorbs the heat energy during daylight and reradiates that heat continually. However, shortly after midday, the ground reaches the local maximum for heat absorption when the sun has passed its period of maximum solar input. This is when the ground radiates the most heat, and air parcels can rise with greater ease. If the temperature of the air parcel remains higher than the surrounding air through which it is rising, an instability results. If the conditions for surface heating of air remain favorable, packets will continue to contribute to the upwelling of air. If the packets of air contain water vapor, the *cumulus stage* of the thunderstorm will begin.

The rising air packets form the basis of the thunderstorm, which is referred to as the thunderstorm cell. As the air packets continue to move upward, the rising column of air causes a pressure imbalance near the surface. This pressure imbalance pulls more air into the system and strengthens the thunderstorm cell. When the rising air reaches its condensation level, a cumulus cloud begins to form as the water vapor condenses out. The act of condensation releases latent heat energy from the water molecules, and this latent heat contributes to the overall energy input of the storm and fuels its growth.

At some point in the process, the resulting cumulus cloud has an enormous store of water, both as water vapor and as water molecules that have condensed out of the system. Water tends to condense out of a cloud system faster when it can form around particulate matter. As the water content of the cloud increases, the condensed water molecules themselves form the seed matter around which other water vapor can condense. The growth of raindrops or ice crystals in the cloud continues in this manner until they are too heavy for the updrafts to support. At this point, the raindrops begin to fall.

The downward motion of the rain causes air in the system to travel downward as well. As the amount of rain increases, the amount of air traveling with it also increases. The storm now enters the second portion of its life cycle, the *mature stage*. At this point, there are two distinct air currents: the updraft caused by the initial formation process and the downdraft caused by the downward motion of the rain.

If sufficient energy is contained in the storm, it is in the mature stage that the updrafts can carry the water and water vapor up as high as 10 or 12 miles until they reach the tropopause, although heights of about 5 miles are more typical. When they reach their maximum elevation, the top of the tower rises no further and is carried in one direction or another by predominant winds at that altitude. As with a squall line storm system, the now-mature cumulonimbus cloud has developed an anvil.

The length of time the storm rages depends entirely on how much energy the thunderstorm contains. As the air hits the ground, it spreads out in all directions. Eventually, the momentum of the spreading downdraft overwhelms the momentum of the updraft, and the source of the air to the thunderstorm cell is cut off. The storm now enters its third and final phase, the *dissipation stage*. It is at this point that the thunderstorm consists almost entirely of downdraft rain. Data from the Thunderstorm Project indicates that only 20% of the water taken into the storm via updrafts is actually returned to the earth in the form of rain. Eventually, the system expends all of its energy, the cumulo-nimbus cloud dissipates, and the summer skies become clear once again.

Thunder and lightning are the hallmark of a thunderstorm, and a summer evening can be spent watching and listening to the spectacle of the thunderstorm in the distance. Lightning is the result of electrical discharge within the storm system itself. When light-ning is created, the heat of the electrical discharge turns the surrounding air to *plasma*, which is an electrically neutral, superheated gas composed of only ions, electrons, and neutral particles. It takes a great amount of energy to do this, and the resulting plasma reaches a temperature of about $10,000°$ C (or $18,000°$ F). This increase in temperature causes air surrounding the newly formed plasma to expand very rapidly, often within a few millionths of a second (microseconds). This rapid expansion sends pressure waves through the atmosphere, resulting in the clap of thunder heard by an observer.

Above the *$0°$ C thermocline,* or the altitude at which the temperature of the air drops below freezing, the liquid water in the cloud becomes ice crystals and super-cooled water droplets. Ice at this altitude is positively charged, and when it drops below the $0°$ C thermocline to become liquid water droplets, its charge becomes nega-tive. When two regions in the cloud build up sufficient opposite *electrical potentials*, or *voltages*, electrical discharge occurs from the positively charged region to the nega-tively charged region. The result is *in-cloud lightning* or *cloud-to-cloud lightning*, which accounts for nearly 80% of all electrical activity in a storm cell.

The surface of the earth likes to maintain a negative electrical potential. The rea-son for this behavior is beyond the scope of this book, but essentially all points on the globe are struggling to maintain a negative charge. The negative electrical potential in the area of the cloud below the $0°$ C thermocline has an interesting effect on the nega-tive potential of the ground below the cloud. Like charges repel, so the reaction of the negative charge in the ground to the proximity of the greater negative charge in the cloud is for the negative charge in the ground to move away from the cloud. Because objects that are not electrically neutral must have either a negative or positive charge, the area of the ground vacated by negative charge takes on a positive potential.

At this point, the situation has changed: The lower half of the cloud has a negative potential and the ground beneath the cloud has a positive potential. Opposite charges attract, so the negative potential in the cloud begins to discharge toward the ground. This initial discharge is called the *leader.* As the leader approaches the ground, the positive potential of the ground causes a sudden upward current to meet the leader halfway. This upward transfer of electrical energy is called a *return stroke.* If there are several pockets of positive potential close together, the return stroke may occur in several locations and meet at the same leader, and the result is *forked lightning.*

The human mind plays interesting games in an attempt to make sense out of an observed situation. Often, the resulting perceived observation is so strong that it is very difficult to convince ourselves that what we saw—or thought we saw—did not occur. When an electrical discharge between cloud and ground begins, the leader and the return stroke occur at the speed of electron flow through a gaseous medium. The light released from this event reaches us at a speed of nearly 186,000 miles per second. A human's visual system is not designed to pick out details in events that occur within that short of a time frame, so the event appears instantaneous. In an attempt to justify the event it just witnessed, an observer's mind translates the observation of the lightning into a continuous strike of power that begins at a cloud and ends at the ground.

The Life Cycle of a Thunderstorm

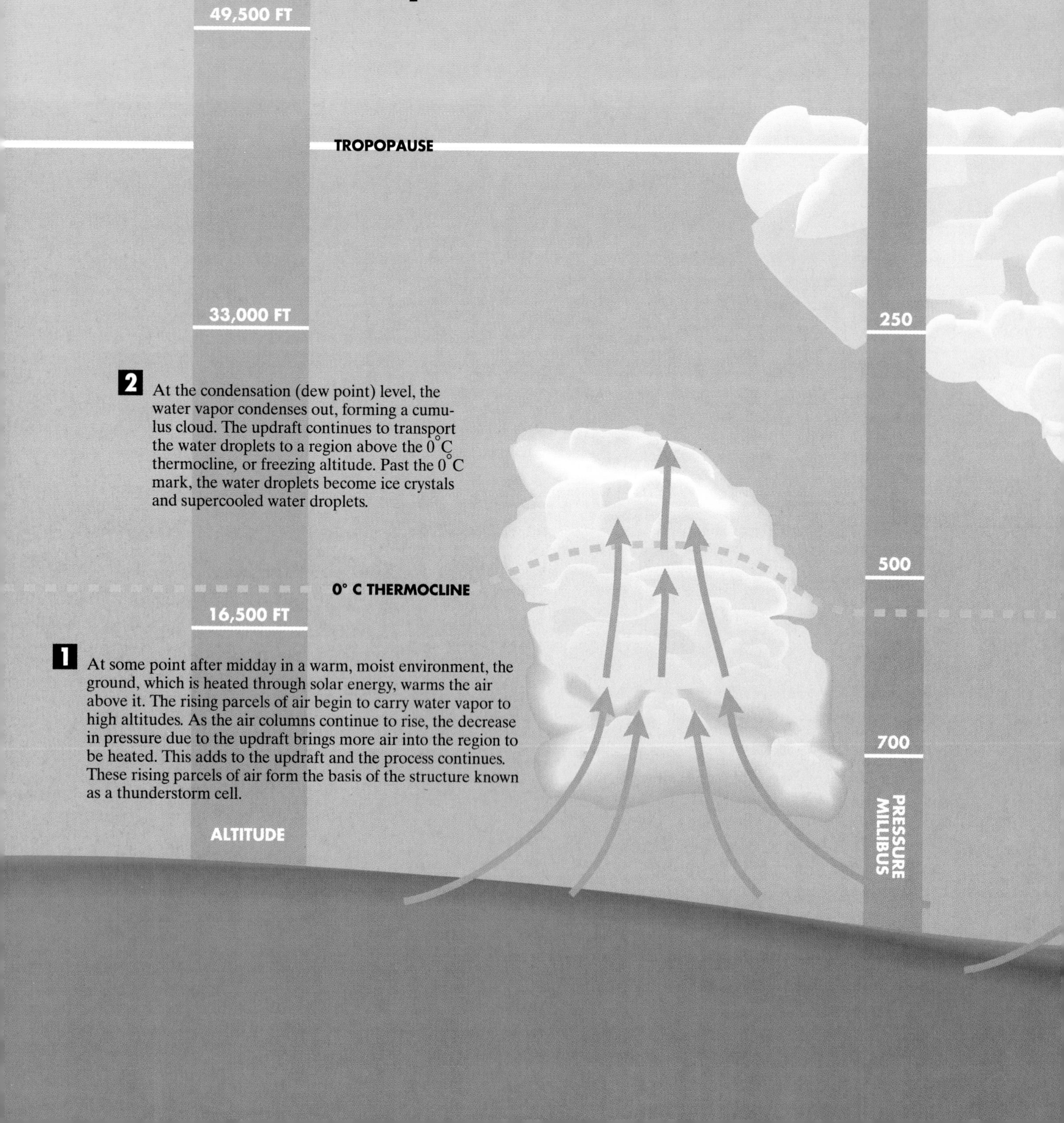

49,500 FT

TROPOPAUSE

33,000 FT

250

2 At the condensation (dew point) level, the water vapor condenses out, forming a cumulus cloud. The updraft continues to transport the water droplets to a region above the 0°C thermocline, or freezing altitude. Past the 0°C mark, the water droplets become ice crystals and supercooled water droplets.

500

0° C THERMOCLINE

16,500 FT

1 At some point after midday in a warm, moist environment, the ground, which is heated through solar energy, warms the air above it. The rising parcels of air begin to carry water vapor to high altitudes. As the air columns continue to rise, the decrease in pressure due to the updraft brings more air into the region to be heated. This adds to the updraft and the process continues. These rising parcels of air form the basis of the structure known as a thunderstorm cell.

700

ALTITUDE

PRESSURE MILLIBUS

3 When the ice crystals and water droplets grow to a size at which the updraft can no longer support their weight, they fall back to the ground in the form of precipitation. The falling water droplets, or raindrops, pull air along with them, causing a strong downdraft within the cell. Now there are two distinct vertical currents of air moving in opposite directions: one up, one down.

4 Because the downdraft has the extra assistance of Earth's gravity, it moves faster than the coexisting updraft. As the air from the downdraft hits the ground, it spreads out and eventually overwhelms the air feeding the updraft. This cuts off the air intake to the storm cell, and eventually the thunderstorm expends all of its remaining energy.

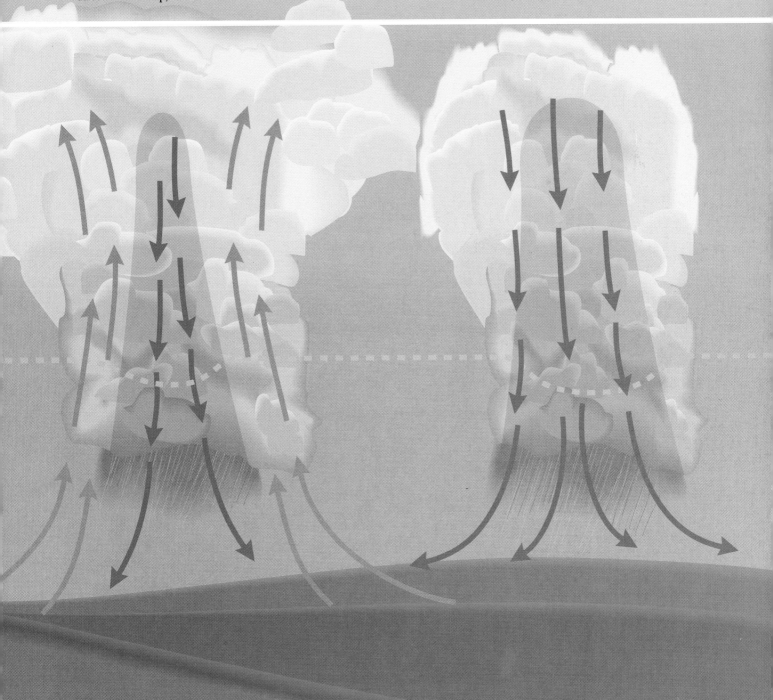

The Structure of Lightning

49,500 FT

33,000 FT

Above the 0° thermocline, ice crystals maintain a positive electric charge. Below the thermocline, water droplets maintain a negative charge.

0° C THERMOCLINE

16,500 FT

In a thunderstorm, 20% of the electrical discharge occurs in cloud-to-ground lightning. The negative potential of the cloud is attracted to the positive potential of the ground. A small filament of charge—called the leader—begins to extend from the cloud to the ground. When the leader is close enough, the positive charge in the ground responds with an immediate discharge of positive charge that meets the leader before it hits the ground. This positive discharge, called the return stroke, completes the lightning cycle.

ALTITUDE

The earth attempts to maintain a negative electrical potential over the entire surface of the planet.

Opposite charges attract. The positive potential of the cloud mass above the thermocline seeks the negative potential of the cloud mass below the thermocline. The result is in-cloud lightning, also called cloud-to-cloud lightning. If the thunderstorm is far enough away that the observer cannot hear the thunder, in-cloud lightning is referred to as heat lightning. In-cloud lightning accounts for 80% of all electrical discharge in a thunderstorm.

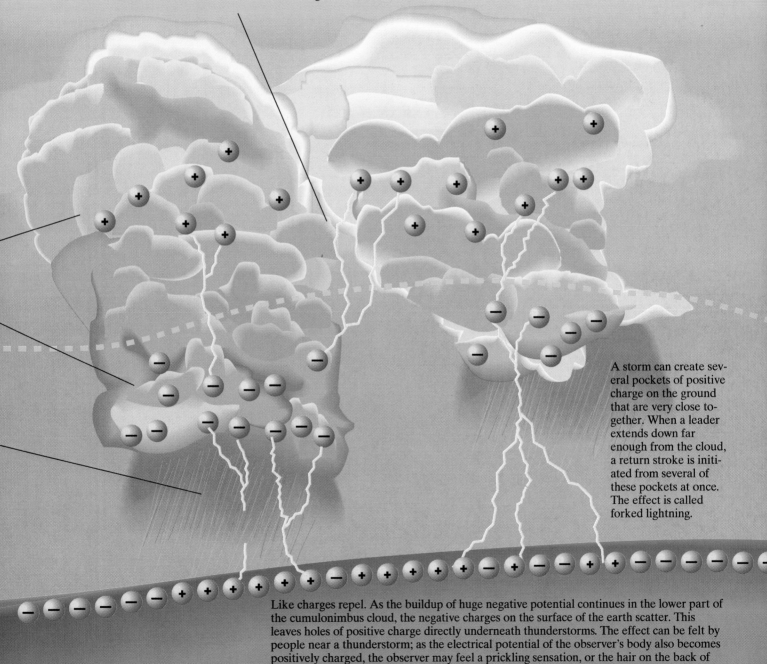

A storm can create several pockets of positive charge on the ground that are very close together. When a leader extends down far enough from the cloud, a return stroke is initiated from several of these pockets at once. The effect is called forked lightning.

Like charges repel. As the buildup of huge negative potential continues in the lower part of the cumulonimbus cloud, the negative charges on the surface of the earth scatter. This leaves holes of positive charge directly underneath thunderstorms. The effect can be felt by people near a thunderstorm; as the electrical potential of the observer's body also becomes positively charged, the observer may feel a prickling sensation, or the hair on the back of the neck standing up. This is because the positive charge in the observer's body is seeking a negative potential so it can discharge. If you feel this sensation, try to become the lowest object in the immediate vicinity, or you could become involved in a lightning flash.

Tornadoes

N THE FALL of 1984, the small community of Barneveld, Wisconsin, was removed from the face of the earth. The town encountered what is, arguably, the weather system's most violent phenomenon: a tornado. Barneveld lay at the northeastern end of the United States's infamous tornado alley, an amorphous region extending roughly from Texas to the Dakotas; the tornado appeared without warning and traveled down the center of town, uprooting trees and destroying buildings. When it was over, the entire community was reduced to rubble.

Barneveld's encounter with the dervish was not unique, and the tornado that traveled through the town was certainly not the most violent, long-lasting, or unpredictable tornado on record. North America experiences roughly 1,000 tornadoes per year, lasting anywhere from a few minutes to the record-holding Mattoon-Charlestown tornado of 1917, which lasted an almost unbelievable 7 hours and 20 minutes. Yet, with all of this opportunity to study tornadoes, advances are only now being made in understanding their origins and behavior. Although meteorologists can alert the population when conditions are favorable for tornadoes, the specifics of the outbreak of a single tornado cannot be predicted with any accuracy. Also, its direction and longevity cannot be determined with anything approaching certainty. Why not?

Even with so many tornadoes in this country, collecting data on them is extremely difficult. They tend to appear and disappear from an area before researchers have a chance to approach them, and the tornadoes have destroyed every wind-speed measurement device placed close enough to gather data. *Tornado chasers* are meteorologists who comb the countryside during favorable tornado conditions in vehicles with cameras, anemometers—devices used to measure wind speed—and other equipment to gain further insight into these twisters. More often than not, the tornado chasers go home empty-handed. Only recently, with the aid of Doppler radar, have meteorologists been able to record a tornado's exact wind speed. Prior to the radar measurements, wind speeds were estimated by examining videos of the debris in the funnel cloud and then performing an analysis of the motion of the debris.

Tornadogenesis is the name given to the process of tornado formation. Although all of the details are not known, meteorologists do have several general ideas as to how the process begins. As tornadoes seem to occur mostly, but not always, when thunderstorms are present, it is logical to assume that the same conditions required for thunderstorm activity (warm, moist environments) are also favored by tornadoes. However, tornadoes are more likely to occur when the conditions are exceedingly moist for the time of year in the region in which they form.

One possible scenario for tornadogenesis begins like this: A temperature inversion (warm air over cold air) is one possible precursor of the beginning of a tornado. Such an inversion prevents heat loss to the upper atmosphere caused by rising warm air, and helps seal in the moisture close to the ground. Above the inversion, the air is dry and warm with a southwesterly wind providing air movement. At the upper altitude region lies a strong westerly wind. Eventually, dynamic lifting causes the moist air to break through the inversion layer and rise to the upper altitudes.

Another idea for the formation of a tornado arose during studies of storm structures in Oklahoma in the mid-1970s. It was postulated that some tornadoes are associated with structures called mesocyclones, which are embedded inside of other, larger storm systems. Mesocyclones are rotating columns of rising air about 15 kilometers (about 10 miles) in diameter.

Mesocyclones form originally in a horizontal position, parallel to the ground: Fast winds in the upper altitudes blow over slower winds moving in the same direction close to the ground. This action creates a situation in which pressure is lower at the upper altitudes than at the lower altitudes and causes a horizontal tube of air to rotate. (The action is similar to the mechanism that provides lift to an aircraft: High-speed winds moving over the top of the wing, creating a lower pressure condition than beneath the wing, force the aircraft to go up.) Once the tube of air is rotating, an updraft, or column of rising air, can force part of the spinning tube to rise, leaving the other end near the ground. We are now left with a situation in which the tube of rotating air is vertical, and a mesocyclone is born. These vertical columns of rotating air may somehow form funnel clouds by providing the spin that is characteristic of a tornado.

Although most meteorologists are now convinced that electrical activity plays no role in the formation, perpetuation, or behavior of a tornado (other than the relationship between a tornado and a thunderstorm), anecdotes of tornadoes coupled with lightning persist, and in fairness they should be mentioned here. The most widely documented anecdote of the coupling of lightning behavior with tornado activity comes from a farmer living near Greensburg, Kansas, on June 22, 1928, who claims to have seen the inside of a tornado funnel while standing at the entrance to his storm cellar.

He reported, "At last, the great, shaggy end of the funnel hung directly overhead. Everything was as still as death. There was a strong, gassy odor and it seemed that I could not breathe. I looked up, and to my astonishment, saw right up into the heart of the tornado. There was a circular opening in the center of the funnel, about 50 to 100 feet in diameter, and extending straight upwards for a distance of at least one-half mile.... The walls of this opening were of rotating clouds and the whole was made brilliantly visible by constant flashes of lightning, which zigzagged from side to side...." (*Monthly Weather Review* 58 [1930]:205)

Like thunderstorms, tornadoes have a life cycle that seems to be characterized by discrete phases: funnel cloud, tornado, mature tornado, shrinking tornado, and decaying tornado. A *funnel cloud* is commonly the observed beginning of a tornado. Extending downward from a cumulonimbus cloud, a funnel cloud is clearly visible as it extends toward the ground. If it ever reaches the ground, it moves into the next phase and is officially designated a tornado. The walls of a tornado are not always visible as condensation vapor (like clouds), but are often defined by the debris and dust that they draw up into the vortex as it hits the ground.

When the tornado funnel reaches its maximum width (anywhere between 15 meters and a couple kilometers) and is nearly perpendicular to the ground, the tornado has moved into its third phase and can be called a mature tornado. A *mature tornado* is a tornado at its most violent, destroying nearly everything in its path. A fast-moving tornado can cross several dozen kilometers before it begins to dissipate. When this happens, the tornado enters into the fourth phase and is labeled a shrinking tornado. The tornado funnel begins to meander and is no longer nearly vertical. In addition, the funnel is significantly reduced in width, and its path of destruction, although erratic, is generally smaller. A *decaying tornado* is small, thin, and distorted—it seems to crawl back up into the sky, leaving devastation in its wake.

The numbers associated with tornadic activity tell the story of their incredible power. An average tornado moves forward at a rate of about 55 kilometers per hour (about 35 miles per hour), and generally moves in a southwest-to-northeast direction. (It is rare that a tornado moves toward the west.) Some tornadoes do reach speeds in excess of 90 kilometers per hour (55 miles per hour), with the record belonging to the March 1925 Tri-State tornado that had a clocked velocity of 117 kilometers per hour (73 miles per hour). Slow moving, or even stationary tornadoes do exist, but they are quite unusual.

Like a skater pulling in her arms during a pirouette, the speed of the winds in a tornado increases as the width decreases. This principle has a name in physics: *the conservation of angular momentum.* Essentially, the total amount of energy in a rotating body tries to remain unchanged during a physical transformation of that body. If a rotating body (a funnel cloud or a skater) retains its mass but decreases its diameter, the body will tend to rotate faster to expend the same amount of rotational energy.

Doppler radar has revealed that the top speeds in the strongest tornadoes are near 450 kilometers per hour (280 miles per hour), with vertical updrafts in the core reaching 290 kilometers per hour (180 miles per hour). The air flow into these tornadoes has been measured at speeds in excess of 180 kilometers per hour (110 miles per hour). The air pressure in an area of a tornado is reduced from the average 14.7 pounds per square inch to about 12.5 pounds per square inch.

The atmosphere produces several types of *wind vortices*, the class of winds to which the tornado belongs. Some of these vortices are related to tornadoes, and others are not. One subclass of wind vortices that people confuse as being a minitornado is the *dust devil*, or *whirlwind*. A dust devil is common sight in warm, dry, calm wind areas where there are large, open plains or deserts. The ground is heated by the noonday sun, and a strong convection begins causing dust and debris to rise, swirling into the air. Dust devils are not only harmless, they are amusing to watch as their behavior can be quite unpredictable. (A common game among children in the southwestern United States is to try to catch dust devils by running into the center of them. When the child enters the vortex, the convection process is cut off and the dust devil dies.)

A *waterspout* is a caused by a rapidly whirling column of air over a body of water. Some forms of waterspouts truly are tornadoes that happen to drift over a lake or river, and others are wind vortices with tornado characteristics that form on their own. The wind velocity inside of a waterspout usually drops to zero when the spout crosses onto land, but there have been cases of waterspouts traveling a far distance inland. Some waterspouts have been reported as carrying fish, frogs and other water-dwelling creatures inland, where they are suddenly dropped on an unsuspecting populace. The phenomenon of a street full of fish is well documented, and though it has never been completely linked to waterspouts, it seems like as good an explanation as any other mechanism.

There is a certain mystery surrounding the creation and behavior of tornadoes that has fascinated people for as long as history has recorded their existence.

Eventually, research will blow away the shroud of mystery, but the fascination will no doubt remain. Regardless of the loss of life and property that a tornado can cause, it is still an amazing occurrence to witness. Those who have unexpectedly experienced a tornado report the event with a mixture of awe and fear, and those who chase tornadoes for a living do so for the love and thrill of seeing one of nature's most powerful creations up close.

The Anatomy of a Tornado

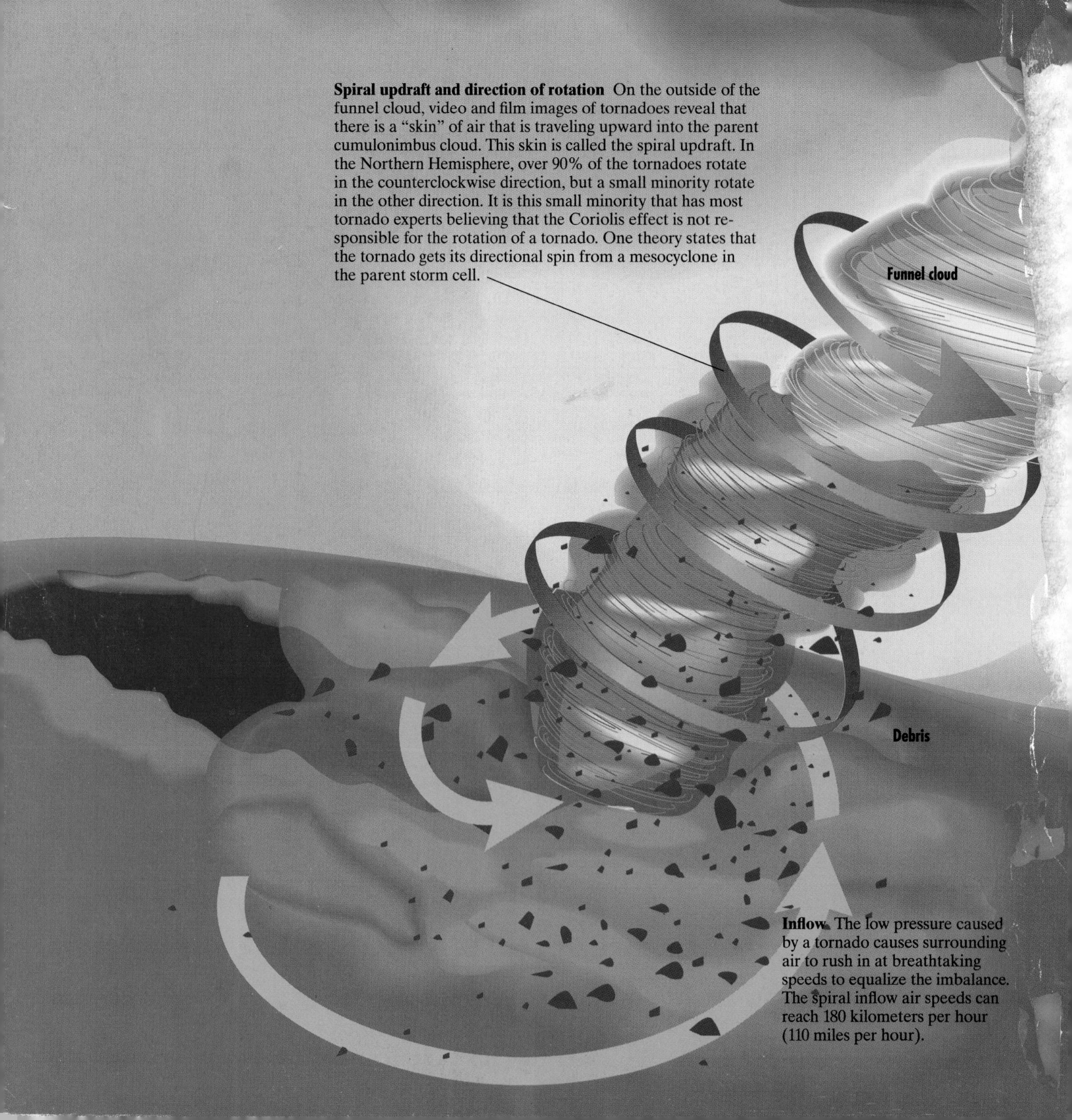

Cumulonimbus cloud

Spiral updraft and direction of rotation On the outside of the funnel cloud, video and film images of tornadoes reveal that there is a "skin" of air that is traveling upward into the parent cumulonimbus cloud. This skin is called the spiral updraft. In the Northern Hemisphere, over 90% of the tornadoes rotate in the counterclockwise direction, but a small minority rotate in the other direction. It is this small minority that has most tornado experts believing that the Coriolis effect is not responsible for the rotation of a tornado. One theory states that the tornado gets its directional spin from a mesocyclone in the parent storm cell.

Funnel cloud

Debris

Inflow The low pressure caused by a tornado causes surrounding air to rush in at breathtaking speeds to equalize the imbalance. The spiral inflow air speeds can reach 180 kilometers per hour (110 miles per hour).

Cumulonimbus cloud The tornado extends down from a typical cumulonimbus cloud that is part of a larger storm system. The cloud may be housing a mesocyclone higher in the cloud tower. The spin of the tornado could be emanating from that mesocyclone. The base of the cumulonimbus can be as low as 300 meters, or about 1,000 feet.

(Image Courtesy of the University of Michigan's Weather Underground Project)

Funnel cloud The funnel cloud is the most distinguishing feature of a tornado. As the tornado begins, the funnel cloud slowly descends out of the belly of the cumulonimbus cloud. Most funnels never reach the ground, but once they do, they are officially classified as tornadoes. The width of the funnel cloud determines the size of the path of destruction and gives evidence as to the strength of the tornado. In its mature phase, the funnel cloud is nearly vertical, and often short and squat. As the tornado begins to decay, the funnel cloud loses much of its girth and begins to meander underneath the cumulonimbus cloud.

Debris A cloud of debris nearly always surrounds the base of a tornado. This upwelling of destruction from the ground is lifted to great heights by the tornado before being released. The air circulation patterns near the base of the tornado are in tremendous disarray, and are responsible for many of the strange stories heard about tornadoes: lifting cows unharmed onto roofs of houses, driving single strands of straw through telephone poles, and so on. Air currents around the base of the tornado range in velocity from 150 to 400 kilometers per hour (90 to 250 miles per hour).

Ted Fujita of the University of Chicago studied wind vortices intently. The Fujita-Pearson Tornado Intensity Scale is a scheme for classifying tornadoes based on wind intensity and path length. Based on a survey of some 20,000 tornadoes, approximately 62% were of weak intensity, 35% were strong, and 3% were violent. The majority of tornado fatalities occurred in violent intensity tornadoes.

Tornado path A recent study revealed that 87% of all tornadoes in the United States move toward the northeast. However, tornadoes moving in all directions (including zigzag and circular paths), and even stationary tornadoes, have been reported. The path of destruction of a tornado varies: About 50% of all tornado paths are less than 90 meters (100 yards) wide, although a few tornadoes have been reported with paths over 1.5 kilometers (1 mile) in width. An average tornado touches down and dies within 15 minutes, leaving the average length of the path to be 14 kilometers (9 miles). However, some tornadoes build up a huge head of steam and can travel for hundreds of miles. The incredibly long-lived Mattoon-Charleston tornado of 1917 traveled a record 471 kilometers (293 miles).

Fujita-Pearson Tornado Intensity Scale					
SCALE	CATEGORY	FORCE (KPH/MPH)	PATH LENGTH (K/MILES)	PATH WIDTH (METERS/YARDS)	EXPECTED DAMAGE
F0	Weak	65–116/ 40–72	0–1.6/ 0–1	0–16 meters/ 0–17 yards	Light
F1	Weak	117–180/ 73–112	1.6–5/ 1–3.1	16–50 meters/ 18–55 yards	Moderate
F2	Strong	182–253/ 113–157	5.1–15.9/ 3.2–9.9	51–160 meters/ 56–175 yards	Considerable
F3	Strong	254–332/ 158–206	16–50/ 10–31	161–508 meters/ 176–556 yards	Severe
F4	Violent	333–418/ 207–260	51–159/ 32–99	0.54–1.4 km/ 0.34–0.9 mile	Devastating
F5	Violent	420–515/ 261–318	161–507/ 100–315	1.6–5 km/ 1–3.1 miles	Incredible

Tornado-Prone Areas of the United States

Tornadoes can occur at most any time of year and at almost any location. Tornadoes have been recorded as far north on the North American continent as Alaska, and at least one was mistakenly classified as a snow devil because its debris cloud was full of snow. However, all areas of the world have tornado windows—when the appearance of tornadoes is most likely.

This data set was gathered in Michigan during the years 1951 to 1986. In the bar graph, the peak months of midsummer can be clearly seen, with nearly zero tornadoes occurring in the winter months. In the path chart, the southwest-to-northeast tendency of tornado paths is apparent, as well as the distribution of tornado strength. (Data courtesy of the University of Michigan's Weather Underground Project.)

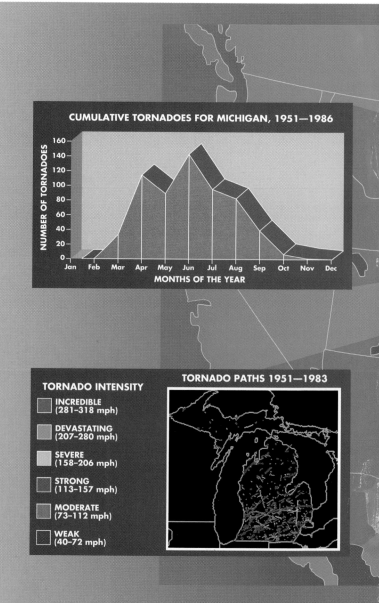

CUMULATIVE TORNADOES FOR MICHIGAN, 1951—1986

NUMBER OF TORNADOES

160 —
140 —
120 —
100 —
80 —
60 —
40 —
20 —
0 —

Jan Feb Mar Apr May Jun Jul Aug Sep Oct Nov Dec

MONTHS OF THE YEAR

TORNADO PATHS 1951—1983

TORNADO INTENSITY

- INCREDIBLE (281–318 mph)
- DEVASTATING (207–280 mph)
- SEVERE (158–206 mph)
- STRONG (113–157 mph)
- MODERATE (73–112 mph)
- WEAK (40–72 mph)

The central and north central areas of the United States are commonly referred to as tornado alley, because the majority of tornadoes in the United States appear in this region. The actual boundary of the region varies depending on whom you consult, but the general area runs from Texas up through the Dakotas and Minnesota. The tornado period for tornado alley runs from April through late June or early July.

The northeastern United States has its periods of peak activity during the humid months of July and August.

In the southeastern United States, the tornado window runs from April through May, with the exception of Florida's main tornado period being June and Mississippi's having plenty of twisters as early as February.

Hurricanes—The Atmosphere's Largest Event

O N AUGUST 23, 1992, a tropical storm in the middle of the Atlantic Ocean developed strong enough winds to be upgraded to a hurricane. The first of the season, Andrew slammed into the eastern coast of South Florida in the early-morning hours of August 24, and maintained enough momentum to cross the width of the state and enter the Gulf of Mexico. The estimated cost of the property damage left in the wake of the hurricane was close to a billion dollars, and the cost of human life, although small by natural-disaster standards, was incalculable to the victims' families. The President declared the region a national disaster area shortly after the storm passed.

A line of thunderstorms, downpours, and spawned tornadoes advanced ahead of Andrew, extending its reach far beyond the state of Florida. Although Andrew hit a bull's-eye with its trajectory, it was nowhere near the most deadly of hurricanes or the most costly in terms of human life. In August 1991, Hurricane Bob struck the eastern seaboard of the United States. When it was still in the middle of the Atlantic, Bob was labeled the most powerful storm that the earth could produce, but by the time it arrived, much of its fury had been diminished. On September 8, 1900, a hurricane made landfall at the small resort town of Galveston, Texas. By the time the hurricane retreated inland, over 10,000 casualties of the storm were reported, 6,000 from Galveston alone.

If a tornado is the most violent atmospheric effect that Earth's weather system can produce, a hurricane is definitely the largest. The rotation of Earth, heat from the sun, and energy input from the ocean and from high-altitude low-pressure troughs all conspire to produce a storm that expends enough energy in one day to provide the United States with energy for a week. The actual size of a hurricane varies from storm to storm, but it is at least several hundred miles in diameter. The surface winds of the front of a hurricane can exceed 160 kilometers per hour (100 miles per hour). The actual influence of a hurricane often extends much farther, producing storm fronts, tornadoes, and inclement weather for hundreds of miles beyond the confines of the hurricane itself. A hurricane, once fully formed, can last for days or weeks.

Hurricanes are classified as *tropical cyclones*, a classification that also includes cyclones and typhoons. All three of these storms are essentially the same, with only the nomenclature changing from region to region. A tropical cyclone off the southeastern United States coastline is referred to as a hurricane; a storm of the same size and strength in the western North Pacific Ocean is called a typhoon; and such a storm in the South Pacific is a cyclone.

The birth of tropical cyclones—like that of tornadoes—is not fully understood. Unlike tornadoes, meteorologists are more keenly aware of the conditions that must be present for a tropical cyclone to be called into existence. Hurricanes begin their lives as *tropical depressions*, strong tropical storms resulting from a high-altitude trough of low pressure. The current estimate is that one out of every two or three depressions develops into a tropical cyclone. One of the requirements seems to be that the tropical depression must be formed very close to the equator, where it can gather the most energy from heated ocean water. It cannot, however, form too close to the equator, as passing from the Northern to the Southern Hemisphere would have a negative effect on the cyclonic activity of the winds in the depression. (Remember that the Coriolis effect causes the inflow winds to rotate counterclockwise in the North and clockwise in the South.)

The temperature of the ocean waters between the latitudes 5° N and 15° N in the Northern Hemisphere, and 5° S and 15° S in the Southern Hemisphere is around 27° C (or 80° F) in late summer. It is in the Hadley Cell—the region within 30° latitude on either side of the equator—where surface winds blow to the west in the North, and east in the South because of the Coriolis effect. As the tropical depression grows in strength inside of this region, the storm system begins a westerly migration. When it passes over these warmer waters, the low pressure in the upper atmosphere causes rising convective air currents, cloud formations, and other instabilities. As this occurs, more and more warm, moist air ascends to the higher altitudes, increasing the size of the low-pressure system dramatically. As the wind speed of the depression passes the threshold of 61 kilometers per hour (or 38 miles per hour) the depression is officially upgraded to a tropical storm.

The rapid pressure decrease in the area of the depression causes the movement of more and more air in toward the center of the depression. As the air approaches the region, the Coriolis effect diverts the airflow into a counterclockwise direction in the Northern Hemisphere, or a clockwise direction in the Southern Hemisphere. As the storm system grows in size, this Coriolis deviation of the airflow causes the clouds to arrange themselves in the roughly spiral pattern that has become the signature for a storm of this type.

The convective updrafts transport more and more moist air from the surface to the top of the storm. When the moisture-laden air reaches its condensation level, the water vapor condenses out and latent heat is released to add energy to the storm system. As the tropical storm increases in size, its low-pressure core pulls more and more air into the system. As with a tornado, the conservation of angular momentum takes effect: When the spiraling winds approach the center of the storm they must move faster to maintain their angular momentum. As the surface wind speeds hit a sustained velocity of 119 kilometers per hour (74 miles per hour) or higher, the tropical storm officially becomes a mature tropical cyclone.

Under normal conditions, the cyclone will stay in the low- to mid-latitude belt of winds out of which it was born. The upper latitudes are normally cut off from the cyclone by a high-pressure zone that is found at the intersection of the Hadley and Ferrel Cells. However, if a low-pressure trough from the upper latitudes extends into the path of the cyclone, it can push through the high-pressure region and steer the cyclone into a northwesterly path in the Northern Hemisphere, or a southwesterly path in the Southern Hemisphere. Depending on the energy in the cyclone, it can travel hundreds or thousands of miles into the upper latitudes.

When a cyclone makes landfall, it is normally cut off from its supply of warm, moist air. Eventually, the storm system will lose its cohesiveness and the cyclone will fall apart. Depending on the size and energy in the cyclone, it may travel many hundreds of miles inland before this happens. And once the cyclone itself is broken down, many storm systems spawned by the cyclone may remain for days.

The structure of a full-blown hurricane, typhoon, or cyclone is well defined. The height of the storm reaches from sea level to about 50,000 feet, or just above the tropopause. Below the 10,000-foot level, there is an inward flow of low-level winds that helps to feed the cyclonic activity of the storm. The innermost band of clouds forms the eye of the storm, or *eye wall*. Inside the eye wall, the wind speeds drop to nearly zero, but the pressure remains subnormal. The eye extends up to the top of the storm, and clear sky can be seen directly overhead. The eye can be 10 to 20 kilometers in diameter, and the cyclonic activity of the eye wall can be clearly seen by observers on the ground.

The season for tropical cyclones is about six months long; the peak is the period in the particular hemisphere when the waters near the equator are the warmest. Due to heat lag, this normally occurs a few months after the astronomical beginning of summer for the region. Hurricane season in the North Atlantic, for instance, reaches its peak around mid-September and can continue as late as early November.

Until the advent of geosynchronous Earth observation satellites, which are satellites that remain stationary with respect to a given point on the earth, not much was known about tropical cyclones. Since their path is steered by aloft winds that are relatively weak, their course can appear erratic. As such, they are impossible to track without the aid of satellites. Furthermore, as these storms are formed well out to sea, before they were detectable by satellite, they were born in privacy, making themselves known only as they approached a populated area. Today, these storms are discovered when they are still tropical depressions, and their speed, strength, and trajectory are monitored very closely.

More than any other single factor, this ability to alert the public days in advance of an approaching tropical cyclone has resulted in the prevention of loss of life in western countries. The death toll of hurricanes in the United States will never again approach the 10,000-plus number of Galveston at the turn of the century. However, throughout the world, the populations of underdeveloped countries are still at risk due to inadequate means of alerting the public. In 1993 alone, deaths due to typhoons totaled over 10,000 people, whereas hurricane victims numbered less than 100.

Wind and Pressure Dynamics of a Hurricane

5 The hurricane itself is not the only cause of damage. On the advancing side of the storm, smaller thunderstorms, tornadoes, and other inclement weather can be generated.

ALTITUDE

15 km

12 km

9 km

6 km

3 km

6 At the center of the storm is the eye of the hurricane, that is, wind speeds drop to nearly zero. However, the pressure differential powering the hurricane is still in evidence as the pressure drops to far below normal for sea-level pressure. Looking up through the eye of a hurricane, an observer would see clear, cloudless skies.

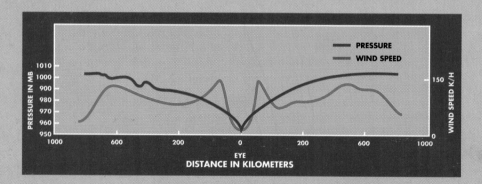

PRESSURE
WIND SPEED

PRESSURE IN MB.
1010
1000
900
980
970
960
950

WIND SPEED K/H
150
0

1000 600 200 0 200 600 1000
EYE
DISTANCE IN KILOMETERS

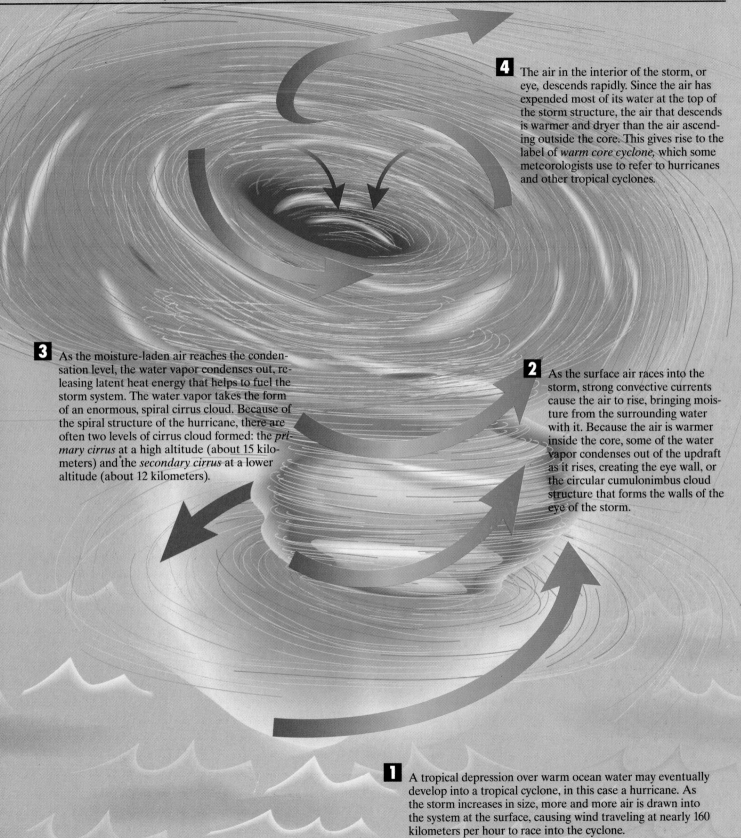

4 The air in the interior of the storm, or eye, descends rapidly. Since the air has expended most of its water at the top of the storm structure, the air that descends is warmer and dryer than the air ascending outside the core. This gives rise to the label of *warm core cyclone,* which some meteorologists use to refer to hurricanes and other tropical cyclones.

3 As the moisture-laden air reaches the condensation level, the water vapor condenses out, releasing latent heat energy that helps to fuel the storm system. The water vapor takes the form of an enormous, spiral cirrus cloud. Because of the spiral structure of the hurricane, there are often two levels of cirrus cloud formed: the *primary cirrus* at a high altitude (about 15 kilometers) and the *secondary cirrus* at a lower altitude (about 12 kilometers).

2 As the surface air races into the storm, strong convective currents cause the air to rise, bringing moisture from the surrounding water with it. Because the air is warmer inside the core, some of the water vapor condenses out of the updraft as it rises, creating the eye wall, or the circular cumulonimbus cloud structure that forms the walls of the eye of the storm.

1 A tropical depression over warm ocean water may eventually develop into a tropical cyclone, in this case a hurricane. As the storm increases in size, more and more air is drawn into the system at the surface, causing wind traveling at nearly 160 kilometers per hour to race into the cyclone.

Typical Tropical Cyclone Paths

During any given year, 50 or so tropical depressions are formed near the equatorial region of the earth. About one-half to one-third of these depressions develop into full-blown tropical cyclones. This chart shows the general birthplace of the storms, and typical paths that tropical storms and cyclones follow. The numbers indicate the approximate number of tropical storms that develop in that region over a one-year period. *(Based on a chart from Dunn and Miller,* Atlantic Hurricanes, *Louisiana State University Press, 1960.)*

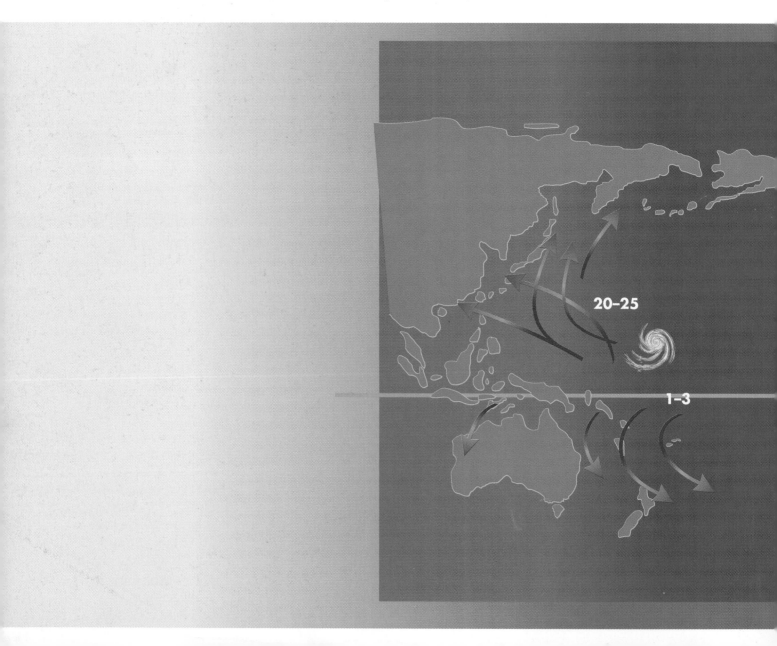

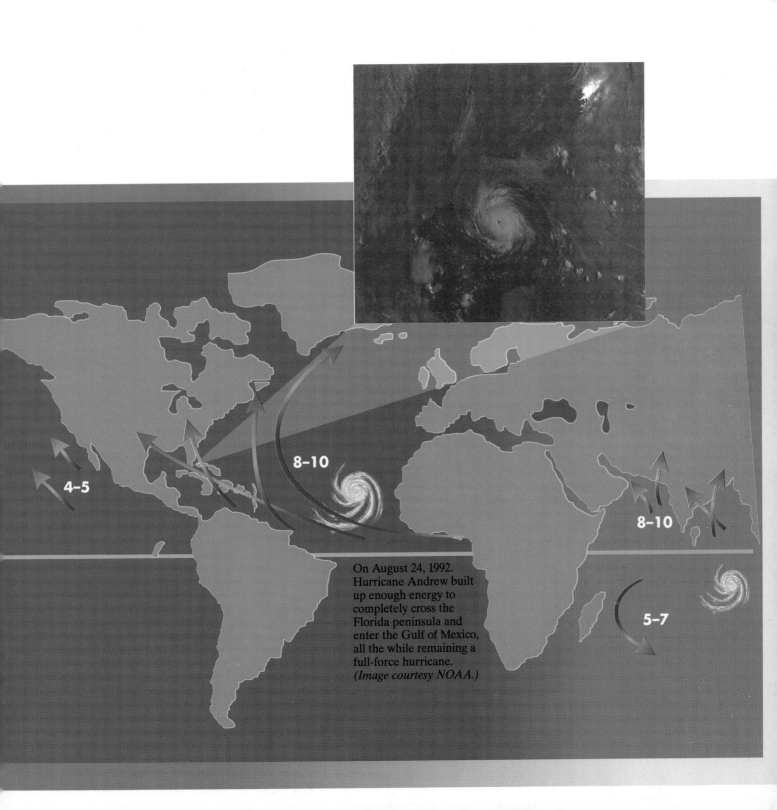

On August 24, 1992.
Hurricane Andrew built
up enough energy to
completely cross the
Florida peninsula and
enter the Gulf of Mexico,
all the while remaining a
full-force hurricane.
(Image courtesy NOAA.)

5

MICROCLIMATES AND UNUSUAL NATURAL PHENOMENA

CONTENTS

WE HAVE LOOKED at the atmosphere of the earth on large scales of time and size. Looking back into the earth's past gives us glimpses of its possible future. Examining air motions on a planetary scale gives us some insight into what the weather might be a day or a week in the future. Tracking storm systems of synoptic scale can help humans save lives and property. These are events that we can grasp, because all the pieces fit, and everything makes sense.

However, as we begin to narrow down our time and distance scales, the world becomes a little more shaky, a little more unpredictable. Focusing on atmospheric events that are only a few tens of kilometers in size, we tend to lose our focus on the bigger picture. These mesoscale and small-scale events seem random—almost maniacal in intent. How else could anyone explain why an airplane is suddenly swatted out of the sky, or the cool, refreshing breezes of the seacoast are kept at bay outside of a city?

Meteorologists have coined the term *microclimate* to refer to local climatological conditions between the earth's surface and an indeterminate altitude where the influence of the earth's global climate overwhelms the influence of the local climate. Although the climatological influence of a large region, such as a city, extends over a greater distance than the word microclimate implies, the term has been expanded to apply to local weather conditions that are distinct from the regional weather patterns.

On an even smaller scale, perhaps even as small as a few meters, the atmosphere can seem almost playful as it jests with us. As the sails are furled in the early evening hours, a sailor spies a glow from the top of the masts. By the time he gets his comrades, the glow is gone. Later, when he is alone again, it is his hand that begins to glow. What small, prankish elf is behind events such as these?

There is no malicious intent to the glow of St. Elmo's Fire. There are no spirits playing with us as we try to fathom nature. We have merely forgotten to take the larger picture into account because these happenings seem so localized, and so personal. In reality, we have merely lost our focus. As we examine the larger picture, the pieces once again fit into place. Lights floating over a swamp are not spirits in the bog, and we begin to welcome these strange occurrences as interesting side effects of living on a dynamic planet. There are no random acts of violence that knock down aircraft, only understandable consequences of physical laws that we must somehow detect and manipulate.

The world becomes far more interesting when it is examined through the lens of understanding rather than through the foggy glass of fear and confusion.

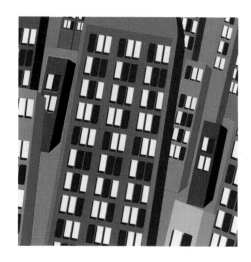

CHAPTER

15

Why Is It Hot in Boston and Cool in Lexington?

ALTHOUGH BOSTON and Lexington are separated by only 19 kilometers (12 miles), the temperature differences between the two areas can be as vast as 5° to 10° C (9° to 18° F). This phenomenon is not limited to cities; it also includes regions where the altitude, surface makeup, or proximity to a large body of water varies over a short distance. The temperature at the top of a mountain, for instance, differs substantially from the temperature at the base of the mountain, even though the two locations may be separated horizontally by only 1 or 2 miles.

In addition, no two places have the same climate, even though they may seem, at first glance, to have similar properties. Although the average yearly temperature of New York, St. Louis, and San Francisco differs by only 1°C (1.8°F), and all three cities reside nearly at the same latitude, the monthly temperature fluctuations of each city differ wildly. (San Francisco varies month to month from its yearly average by only 5°C; New York varies from its yearly average by as much as 12°C.)

San Francisco's temperature is greatly moderated by its location near the ocean. The city is east of the Pacific, and the prevailing winds blow from west to east in the latitude of San Francisco. San Francisco, then, receives a great deal of its temperature influence from the sea and is said to have a *marine climate.* St. Louis, on the other hand, is nearly in the center of the North American continent. Areas where local climate is not influenced greatly by large bodies of water are said to have a *continental climate.* New York, though a coastal city, also receives much of its weather due to the influence of the troughs of the polar jet stream, which brings cooler air down into the region during the winter months.

That is why city climates differ from each other, but why do climates of the city and its surrounding area vary so much? Cities essentially modify their own local climate conditions. As a city grows in size, the landscape is slowly denuded of foliage and soil. This natural ground cover is replaced by tar, asphalt, and concrete, which are more efficient heat sinks than soil and vegetation, and large buildings are erected that intrude on the passage of air. These human modifications result in a local climate that is significantly different from that of the surrounding landscape.

This condition has been called the heat-island effect, because the climate of a city is as different from the climate of its surroundings as the climate of an island is from the water in which it is situated. In the late 1960s and early 1970s, researchers at the University of Maryland monitored the local temperature conditions in and around a small town in Maryland as it grew from 200 to over 20,000 inhabitants. The mean temperature of the area increased steadily as the population increased.

Solar radiation falls on a city and its surrounding countryside in equal amounts. In the countryside, there is a normal distribution of energy absorbed and energy reradiated. For the city, however, the situation is now drastically altered. The total amount of exposed concrete and asphalt allows for greater absorption and heat storage capacity within the city. As such, the city has a greater ability to reradiate the heat as longwave radiation.

In addition, the concrete surface of a city provides for more efficient water runoff than does soil and vegetation. So, there is less water available for evaporation, and, as a result, a city is less humid than the surrounding climate. People often say that humid heat is worse than dry heat, but this is only true when comparing a humid region and an arid region of the same temperature. Evaporation requires energy, which is absorbed from solar energy. Essentially, heat is removed from a system via evaporation; this is why people feel cooler on a hot day when they are sweating. Without the available supply of water for evaporation, more of the solar energy falling on a city is absorbed by the concrete. The result is that the temperature of the city stays warmer longer; during a hot summer, a large city can remain uncomfortably warm long into the night.

Computer models and climatological studies are showing other ways in which large cities affect the local climate. Even though cities are less humid than the surrounding countryside, recent studies are showing that summer rainfalls over and downwind of large urban areas are greater than the rainfall in nearby nonurbanized areas. These computer models are showing that the increased heat output of a city results in increased convection, which could be responsible for increased cloud formation. It is also suspected that the presence of massive skyscrapers is somehow stimulating cumulonimbus cloud growth, but the mechanism involved is not that well understood.

Another mechanism that is not well understood is the interplay between industrial activity and local climates. Clearly, the annual output of millions of tons of carbon monoxide, carbon dioxide, fossil fuels, pollutants, and dioxins into the air changes the local chemistry of the atmosphere. The effects and extent of acid rain on downwind vegetation, for instance, is well known. Does the alteration of the local air chemistry imply that the behavior of the atmosphere and its relationship to local climate are also changing? Probably: Smog conditions in urban areas such as Los Angeles and Mexico City are affecting the amount of heat trapped in these cities by absorbing and then reradiating heat.

Influence of an Urban Area on the Local Climate

Sunlight brings equivalent amounts of solar energy to a woodland area and an urban area that are within several kilometers of each other. The woodland region and the urban region take up the same amount of surface area. Fifty percent of the incoming solar energy makes it through the atmosphere and reaches the surface.

Of the radiation that is absorbed, most of it is reradiated as long-wave radiation fairly quickly because soil and rock have relatively poor heat capacity. The long-wave, or *infrared*, radiation that gets reradiated enters Earth's natural greenhouse effect cycle: Some of the infrared radiation is reflected back to Earth by carbon dioxide in the atmosphere, some is absorbed by water during the natural evaporation process, and a small percentage escapes back into space.

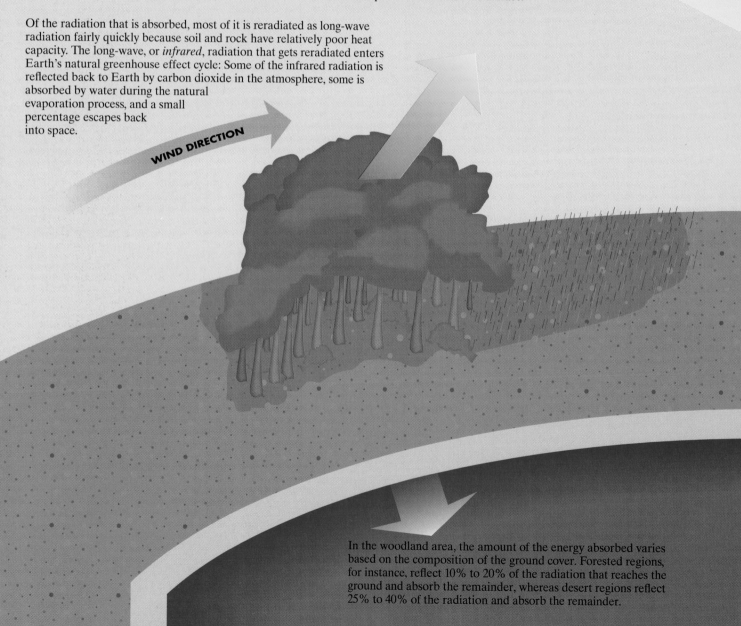

WIND DIRECTION

In the woodland area, the amount of the energy absorbed varies based on the composition of the ground cover. Forested regions, for instance, reflect 10% to 20% of the radiation that reaches the ground and absorb the remainder, whereas desert regions reflect 25% to 40% of the radiation and absorb the remainder.

Recent studies have shown that there is a greater degree of summer rainfall and cloud production over and downwind of urban centers. The reasons for this are not well understood, but some ideas suggest that the presence of skyscrapers and/or increased convection due to prolonged reemission of heat energy play a part in the cloud formation.

In urban areas where pollutants are present, some of the infrared radiation is reflected back to the surface by a layer of smog and carbon dioxide at a lower level. Once again, this keeps more heat in the system.

Although heat energy is reemitted as infrared in the same manner in the urban area as it is in the woodland area, the lack of water in the urban area means that a smaller amount of the heat energy leaves the area because of evaporation. Consequently, more heat stays in the system.

In the urban area, the concrete, asphalt, and cement that constitute the floor of a city have a larger heat capacity than do soil and rock. Consequently, more heat energy is absorbed by a city for reradiation in the infrared. This can lead to a greater overall heat input to the city than to the corresponding woodland area over the course of a day.

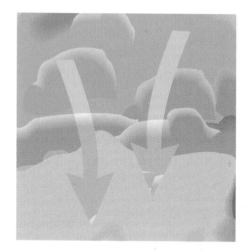

Dangerous Air and Air Travel

I N EARLY APRIL of 1974, a remarkable outbreak of 148 tornadoes occurred near Beckley, West Virginia. The tornadoes left a predictable display of damage in their wake for an outbreak of that size: over 2,500 miles of total damage paths and over 300 people dead. Taking part in an aerial survey of the damage, Dr. Ted Fujita of the University of Chicago took note of twisted trees and wind-damaged lands near the area. He also took note of an interesting display of tree damage that others had seen also, but the meaning of which had been overlooked.

A large cluster of trees had been destroyed in the West Virginia countryside, which was not unusual for a tornado outbreak of this size. What was unusual was the pattern that the trees made: Rather than being twisted and uprooted, this grove of trees was knocked flat, the tops of the trees pointing in a starburst pattern away from a central point. Surveying other sections of the damage from the outbreak, Dr. Fujita noticed this pattern several more times. His conclusion was that in the midst of the tornadoes, another powerful mechanism was at work. The idea did not catch on quickly, and almost no investigation into possible mechanisms was performed.

About one year later, on June 24, 1975, an Eastern Airlines flight into New York's Kennedy airport was knocked to the ground while attempting to land. Once again, Dr. Fujita noticed a starburst shape in the foliage, dust, and debris similar to the wind patterns in West Virginia, recorded near the runways. Putting this information together with data collected over Eastern's flight data recorder, or *black box*, and eyewitness reports, Dr. Fujita concluded that the aircraft encountered a downdraft of air strong enough to knock it down.

Fujita labeled these downdrafts *downbursts* and broke them into two categories: *macrobursts*, which are typically mesoscale-sized events greater than 4 kilometers (2.5 miles) in extent, and *microbursts*, similar events that are less than 4 kilometers in extent. It came to be realized very quickly that microbursts could be responsible for a great deal of unexplained aircraft crashes. Since accurate records started to be kept, a total of 27 microburst-related air travel accidents have been recorded from the late 1970s through 1989 in the United States alone.

Downdrafts are an integral part of the dynamics of thunderstorms and other convective storm systems. Meteorologists had always believed that by the time outflow from a downburst reached the ground, it would be too weak to do any damage. Although this is true most of the time, not enough energy had been invested into modeling the situation to see what other effects might occur. Once serious investigations into the phenomenon began, the true dynamics of downdrafts, and microbursts in particular, began to be revealed.

If the airflow from a downdraft is particularly strong, it hits the surface of the earth with a great deal of force. The effect is similar to taking a water hose and aiming it at the ground: The water contacts the ground, splashes, and rolls out in all directions equally. The same thing happens with a strong downdraft: The air hits the ground and moves away from the center of the downdraft.

As the air moves horizontally over the ground, it rolls away very rapidly, causing high winds and a phenomenon called wind shear—an interface where there is a sudden change in wind direction and velocity. It is wind shear, and not the high wind speeds themselves, that makes microbursts so dangerous to pilots. Depending on the direction from which the aircraft encounters the microburst, the plane will experience a rapid increase in headwind followed immediately by an increase in tailwind. This can produce a rapid drop in altitude of several hundred feet; and when an aircraft is either approaching or departing from an airport, it does not have several hundred feet to spare.

Two varieties of microbursts have been classified: wet and dry. In *wet microbursts*, rain-laden downdrafts occur from a cumulonimbus cloud with a cloud base of about 3,000 feet; this moisture-thick air relies on drier air outside the storm system in order to undergo rapid evaporative cooling. This cooling makes the downdraft air heavier than the surrounding air and it drops even more rapidly. A wet microburst appears as a dark, rain-filled shaft extending down from the storm cloud. If the edges of the microburst can be seen clearly, the "splashing air" effect becomes visible. Wet microbursts, however, are often obscured from the pilot's view by heavy rainfall from the storm itself.

Dry microbursts occur in areas where moist convection is just barely possible, such as the semiarid regions of the southwestern United States. In the dry microburst scenario, the base of the cumulonimbus cloud is quite a bit higher, on the order of 10,000 feet. The downdraft begins as usual, taking moisture along with the air currents. Before the rain reaches the ground, however, it evaporates—this occurs around the 6,000-foot level. (Rain that evaporates before hitting the ground is called *virga* and is common in many arid areas of the world.) This evaporation intensifies the evaporative cooling of the air, which gives more force to the downdraft winds that reach the surface.

In previous chapters we discussed *gust fronts*, or the leading edge of the storm's advancing wedge of cold, downdraft air. The leading edge of the gust front also produces wind shear, but the effect may not be as strong or as rapidly shifting as wind shear from the outflow closer to the microburst's center. (An aircraft encountering a gust front can experience a rapid increase in headwind.) A gust front far from a microburst's center poses less of a threat to an aircraft then does an encounter with the actual microburst.

On March 3, 1991, United Airlines flight 585 slammed into the ground outside of the Colorado Springs airport, killing 25 people. The aircraft was approaching Colorado Springs in relatively clear air, and records of cockpit-to-ground communications revealed nothing unusual. Suddenly, the aircraft tilted violently as though it were in an extreme starboard bank. For 9 seconds, the pilots vainly tried to regain control of the aircraft, but were unsuccessful, and the Boeing 727 hit the ground. Examination of the wreckage did not indicate any mechanical or structural defect. Examinations of the aircraft's flight data recorder and eyewitness accounts did not shed any light on the disaster. The National Transportation Safety Board, or NTSB, still lists the accident as unexplained, something the NTSB has only done once before in its history.

Although it has never been proven with direct evidence, the profile of the United Airlines crash fits the computer model for an aircraft encounter with a *rotor*, a rapidly spinning horizontal tube of air. As a moving cold air mass encounters a topographical feature such as a mountain, its forward momentum carries it up the side of the mountain. As it reaches the top of the mountain, the cold air, assisted by gravity, begins to travel down the other side, picking up speed as it travels. The rotation of the air as it moves down the side of the mountain gives the rotor its name. An aircraft caught in a rotor would experience a strong tendency to roll with the spinning tube of air. To date, no aircraft crashes have been positively identified as being caused by a rotors.

The Federal Aviation Administration, or FAA, has funded a successful project (with the work performed by such organizations as the Weather Sensing Group at the Massachusetts Institute of Technology's Lincoln Laboratory and the National Center for Atmospheric Research in Boulder, Colorado) on the detection of microbursts and gust fronts using Doppler weather radar and the subsequent report of those detections to air traffic personnel and pilots. The first phase of the project, known as Terminal Doppler Weather Radar, or TDWR, began operation in several airports in 1993. The second phase of the project, known as Integrated Terminal Weather System, or ITWS, will expand the project to include many more sensors than TDWR. ITWS is scheduled for deployment before the turn of the century.

An Aircraft Encounter with a Wet Microburst

1 As the aircraft approaches the runway on a normal approach path, the pilot may see heavy rain ahead, but there is nothing unusual to indicate that a problem may be waiting.

NORMAL APPROACH PATH

2 Upon penetrating the microburst, the aircraft encounters increased headwinds by as much as 30 knots to 60 knots (34.5 mph to 69 mph). The increased winds over the wings cause increased lift on the aircraft, and the plane suddenly begins to rise.

3 The very human reaction of the pilot to this situation is to immediately point the nose of the aircraft down to try and stop the rapid altitude increase. At this point, the aircraft may be passing the center of the downburst or just entering the other side of the outflow.

4 Now the aircraft has entered the out-flow opposite the one it originally entered. The aircraft experiences an increased tailwind equal or nearly equal to the strength of the head-wind it just encountered. The pilot, still attempting to compensate for the original altitude increase, has the nose of the plane pointed down as the increased tailwind robs the plane of its newfound lift.

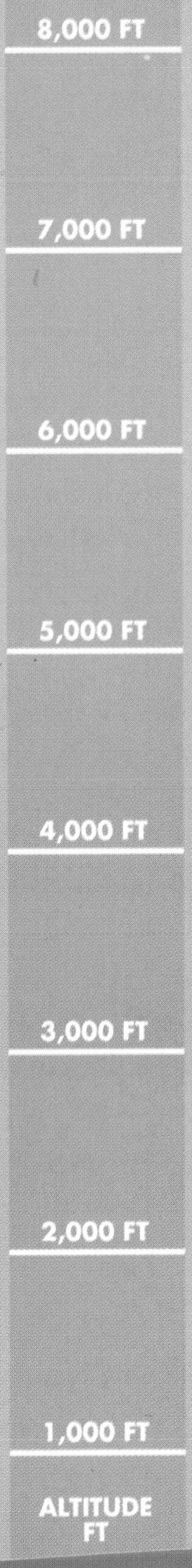

8,000 FT

7,000 FT

Why doesn't a pilot fly around a wet microburst if the rain shaft of the microburst is visible? First of all, not all rain shafts contain microbursts. Also, microbursts are often shrouded inside storm systems, or in lines of storms. Often, rather than routing a plane completely around a storm system that may be a hundred miles long, air traffic controllers route the plane through a perceived break in the storm. The rain shaft of the microburst is often obscured by the rain of the storm system itself. It is in these situations that a plane is most likely to encounter the microburst.

6,000 FT

5,000 FT

4,000 FT

3,000 FT

2,000 FT

5 The result: The plane loses several hundred feet of altitude in just a few seconds. Although planes en route encounter this type of altitude drop all the time, a loss of several hundred feet in altitude when the plane is only several hundred feet above the ground is disastrous.

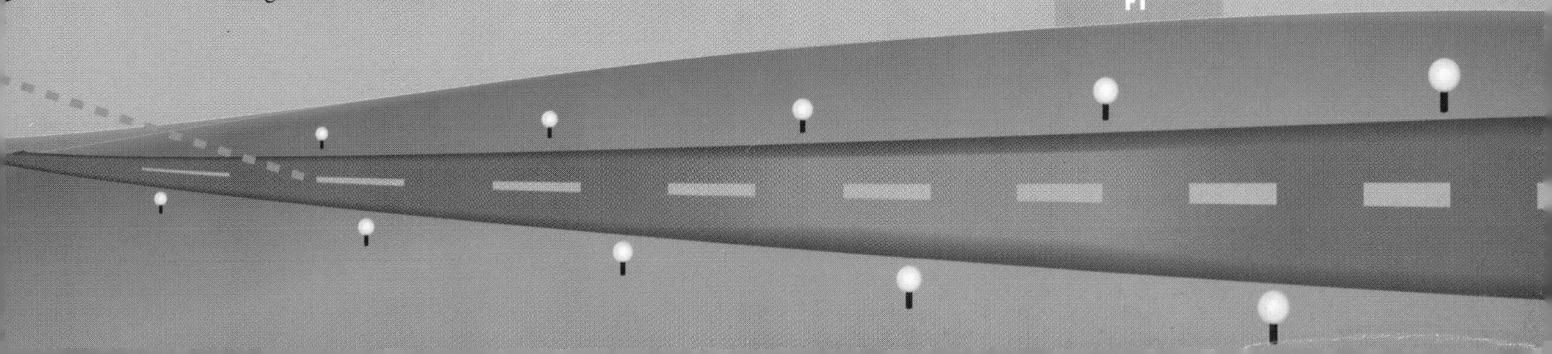

1,000 FT

ALTITUDE
FT

CHAPTER

17

Unusual Weather Phenomena

THE WORLD IS filled with strange tales: stories of creatures living in the lakes of Scotland, strange lights appearing in the sky, and fish raining from the clouds over small, coastal towns. Scientists have treated these stories with less than enthusiasm, often dismissing them offhandedly as folklore. To be fair to the science community, no doubt the majority of these tales are the product of overactive imaginations. Once in a rare while, however, witnesses are able to present objective evidence of an unusual encounter and the world is forced to take note. It is in these cases that turning a deaf ear on the evidence does an incredible injustice to the scientific process. The universe is a vast place where anything is possible.

It is fair to say that only a few of these phenomena are completely understood. It is hard enough to understand a well-documented event like a tornado, let alone an occurrence of ball lightning, St. Elmo's fire, Andes fire, and green flash. These prankish occurrences of nature do not happen very often, or at predictable times. The very nature of their unpredictable and short existence implies that it would be a most remarkable coincidence indeed if a truckload of sensors were to be in the same area in which they occur. Occasionally, however, there is a camera.

Ball lightning appears to be a self-contained globe of electrical discharge and is almost always reported just before or during a large electrical storm. The incidents of ball lightning are so numerous that photographs have been taken of the glowing orbs. Because of the sheer number of reports, including reports from noted meteorologists, the meteorological community has always recognized their existence. The mechanism behind ball lightning, however, is still a complete mystery. The appearance of ball lightning inside closed, metallic structures such as airplane fuselages and hangars may indicate the involvement of *electrical induction*, the generation of electromotive forces by the fluctuation of magnetic fields. But how a self-contained ball of plasma could sustain itself for a prolonged period of time is a complete mystery.

Ball lightning has been reported to range from the size of a pea to several meters in diameter. The physical descriptions of the phenomenon are nearly the same: a central blue-white glowing ball surrounded by a spherical halo of some indeterminate color. Ball lightning has been reported to spontaneously appear "out of thin air" or just to float into the observer's field of vision from somewhere else. The most intriguing aspect of ball lightning is its prankish nature and the fact that no deaths have been associated with it. Ball lightning has been reported to drift in an open window, travel in a circle around astonished onlookers, and leave by the same window.

When ball lightning outstays its welcome (generally from only a few seconds to a minute), eyewitnesses almost always report hearing a pop or violent crashing noise at the instant of disappearance. (Possibly most telling is the large number of reports claiming that the ball disappears when a lightning discharge occurs nearby.) Without exception, every eyewitness of ball lightning has reported an acrid smell, which is undoubtedly ozone produced by electricity, when the apparition is gone.

A lightning-induced phenomenon that is well understood is *St. Elmo's fire*, a blue-to-greenish emanation around objects caused by static electric discharge just before or during a lightning storm. St. Elmo's fire has been noted by William Shakespeare and Herman Melville, and has been a part of sea folklore as long as there have been sailors. Sailors have typically regarded the effect as good fortune, a sign that the ship will be guided through the storm. In reality, St. Elmo's fire is a precursor to a lightning strike.

A negative charge in the lower deck of a cumulus cloud repels a negative charge in the ground, and a positive charge rushes in to take its place. This positive charge is attracted to the negative charge in the cloud and is an integral part of the process of a lightning strike. Because an electrical charge moves easier through solid matter than it does through gas, lightning's return stroke tends to remain in solid matter as long as possible. (This is why it is crucial during an electrical storm to make yourself the lowest point in your immediate surroundings). On the top of a mountain, the process of lightning production is the same, but there are very high places from which the lightning return stroke can begin. On a ship at sea, very often the highest points are the sailors on deck or the ship's masts. The positive charge is attracted to the negative charge in the cloud, and the return stroke begins the process by extending up toward the cloud. The result is a greenish glow around the point of departure, which is called St. Elmo's fire. St. Elmo's fire has been reported to emanate from people's fingertips, mast tops, trees, and telephone poles. A similar phenomenon called Andes fire can be seen around tops of mountain ranges. Andes fire is a scaled-up version of St. Elmo's fire; positive charge collects in the tops of the mountains and glows green as a precursor to a possible return stroke.

Sailors, because they're out at sea, are more keenly aware of the power of nature and are more prone to notice when something unusual has occurred. This may be the reason that sailing folk were the first recorded people to notice a trick of the atmosphere called the green flash. Less than a second after the sun has set on the horizon, people have reported seeing an intense green flash of light that lasts only a moment, and then is gone.

The cause of the green flash is immediately apparent if you remember that light from the sun is really a conglomeration of an infinite number of wavelengths of visible light; humans view each of these different wavelengths as colors. When this conglomeration of wave lengths, or *white light*, is passed through a prism, the various wavelengths composing the light can be clearly seen as a *spectrum*, or distribution of the light energy. (The analysis of the composition of material based on emitted or absorbed light by an object is called spectral analysis.)

The spectrum of white light consists of the entire range of color wavelengths from long-wave, low-frequency red to short-wave, high-frequency violet; green is roughly in the middle of the spectrum. The reason the wavelengths composing the white light can be split up by the glass is related to the amount of energy contained in each wavelength. Red light has the least amount of energy and, as such, is bent the least by the prism, and violet light, which has the most energy, is bent the most.

When conditions are just right, the atmosphere itself acts like a prism. As the sun sets behind the horizon, the energetic light from the sun (the high-frequency light) is bent by the atmosphere around the curve of the earth's surface. Since the human eye is the most receptive to green wavelengths, the effect is momentarily noted on our retinas as a green flash.

The Causes of Two Unusual Phenomena

Although many unusual atmospheric phenomena have been recorded, relatively few have been satisfactorily explained. The reasons for this vary, but have much to do with unusual atmospheric conditions leading up to the phenomena, the rarity of the phenomena, the lack of research or recording equipment at the time of their occurrence, and the anecdotal quality of many of the reports.

St. Elmo's Fire

As a precursor to a lightning strike, a positive charge collects in the ground below a cumulonimbus cloud containing a negative charge. As the leader begins to extend from the cloud, the return stroke, composed of a positive charge, begins to ascend. The positive charge will take a path through solid, conducting matter before it travels through the atmosphere. The sea is basically flat, which means there is a limited amount of matter taller than the surface of the water. In the scenario shown here, the charge travels to the top of a ship's mast and is clearly seen on board the ship as a glow emanating from the masts. The crew themselves may also be glowing around the fingertips or mustaches.

The Green Flash

As the sun sets below the horizon, light from the sun is refracted by the atmosphere back over the horizon. The wavelengths of light from green to violet are refracted the most. Because human vision has evolved to be the most receptive to green wavelengths, an observer on the ground may see a green flash of light just after the sun sets. The flash only lasts for a second.

6
THE ATMOSPHERE OF OUR NEIGHBORS

CONTENTS

T EXTBOOKS OF ONLY 15 years ago were citing differences among Earth and the other planets in the solar system: Earth is the only planet that is geologically dynamic; Earth is the most active atmospherically; Earth is the only planet with weather. The list went on and on. One by one, each of these distinctions has eroded as technology revealed to us planets that we may well be seeing for the first time.

As space probes began whizzing by other planets in the outer solar system, and the satellites of the gas giants loomed into the view of the robot explorers' eyes, it became clear that planets were not the only bodies in the solar system with atmospheres. Titan, one of the moons of Saturn, has a carbon-rich atmosphere that may be similar to the primordial atmosphere of Earth. Surface atmospheric pressure on Titan is 50% greater than the atmospheric pressure on the surface of Earth. Triton, one of the moons of Neptune, has an "atmosphere" composed of frozen nitrogen that is only a few meters thick. Far from being inert, Triton has active volcanoes that replenish the atmosphere with a mixture of frozen and gaseous nitrogen. Europa, one of the moons of Jupiter, does not have an atmosphere in the traditional sense of the word, but instead seems to be covered in an ocean of liquid water that is protected from space by a thick covering of water ice.

Among the planets themselves, weather abounds. Wind vortices, similar to dust devils on Earth, tower several kilometers above the surface of Mars. The thick, sulfuric acid–laden atmosphere of Venus is home to lightning strikes similar to those found on Earth. The Great Red Spot on the surface of Jupiter is an intense atmospheric vortex: a storm many times the size of Earth, which has been raging for thousands, perhaps tens of thousands, of years.

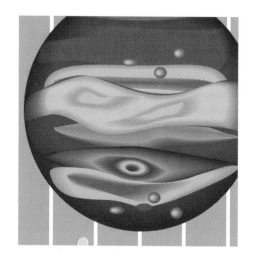

Planetary Atmospheres: Variation on a Theme

OUT OF THE void, all nine planets and a handful of natural satellites developed with some form of an atmosphere. Although all share the basic chemical constituents, the exact composition, density, temperature, state, and dynamics vary considerably from body to body. Some atmospheres are so thin that they are nearly nonexistent; the planet Mercury, for instance, has the killing combination of a weak gravitational field and a close proximity to the sun. It could not maintain most of its gaseous envelope. As a result, Mercury's helium-based atmosphere has a surface pressure of only 1×10^{-11} atmospheres (atms). With pressure that low, the chances of two molecules interacting are highly unlikely: Weather does not occur on Mercury.

Pluto is at the other extreme. Its distance from the sun's heat has lowered its atmosphere's kinetic energy to the point where the gas composing its atmosphere has solidified. Pluto is shrouded in a frozen atmosphere of methane, and its low kinetic energy means that there are almost no dynamics occurring. Pluto, like Mercury, is deprived of weather.

Jupiter, one of the planets classified along with Saturn, Uranus, and Neptune as a *gas giant*, has a radius of 71,900 kilometers, or almost 45,000 miles. (By way of contrast, Earth has a radius of only 6,378 kilometers, or nearly 4,000 miles.) Even though the main components of the Jovian atmosphere are hydrogen and helium, two of the lightest elements, 71,900 kilometers of air takes its toll. Progressing down through the first 100 kilometers (62 miles) of Jupiter's gas envelope, we reach an atmospheric pressure of 1 atm, the average surface atmospheric pressure on Earth. The temperature at this level, which is well into Jupiter's troposphere, is a balmy $-100°$ C $(-148°$ F). Moving down only another 50 kilometers (31 miles) raises both the atmospheric pressure and the atmospheric temperature. At this level, the pressure is 5 atms and it is $0°$ C.

Past this point, Jupiter pushes atmospheric science to its theoretical limit: Although the equations and computer models can take us deep under Jupiter's cloud tops, no laboratory on Earth can simulate the incredible pressures and temperatures required to test out these models. At 8,500 kilometers (5,280 miles) below the top of the atmosphere, the atmospheric pressure reaches 2 million atms. At these pressures, the computer models tell us that the hydrogen would compress itself and change its state from gas to liquid, which would take on true metallic properties: an ocean of liquid metal hydrogen. Progressing down to a level of 57,000 kilometers below the atmospheric surface, the pressure would increase to an unimaginable 45 million atms with a temperature of around 20,000° C to 30,000° C. It is at this level that it is believed an iron-composite solid core exists.

Measurements of the atmosphere down to 150 kilometers below the top of the cloud deck have been taken by the Voyager spacecraft during flybys through the Jovian systems. In 1996, the Galileo spacecraft will take direct measurements of the pressure and temperature profiles of the atmosphere of Jupiter by dropping a probe into the gas giant. The Galileo probe is expected to stay alive for nearly 45 minutes, transmitting data from many hundreds of kilometers below the cloud tops.

The planets Mercury, Venus, Earth, and Mars (occasionally Earth's satellite, the Moon, is included in this list) are classified as the *terrestrial planets*. Of these bodies, only Venus, Earth, and Mars have dynamic atmospheres where weather occurs. Even among these three, however, the composition and dynamics of their atmospheres differ tremendously. Prior to the advent of planetary exploration, Venus, our Morning Star, was an enigma. Its thick, cloudy atmosphere lent mystery and intrigue to the planet. Because it was close to the sun, people believed that Venus was hotter than Earth, and its cloud-covered surface led people to believe that it also contained more water. The surface of Venus, it was thought, must surely be covered with swampland.

As remote-detection techniques improved, Soviet spacecraft began to rain down upon the surface of Venus, U.S. spacecraft orbited the planet with radar and atmospheric sensors, and the real story began to unfold. The average planetary surface temperature on Venus is nearly 460° C, or just over 850° F, and the surface pressure is in excess of 90 atm. Very little water exists in the Venusian atmosphere. Venus is nearly the same size as Earth, so gravitational compression could not account for the temperature and pressure discrepancy; and Venus's distance from the sun should have raised the average surface temperature above Earth's by only 25° C. So what happened?

One explanation is that when Venus and Earth formed from the accretion disk, their positions relative to the sun were nearly the same: Venus's orbit is 71% of the radius of Earth's orbit. Because of their proximity inside of the original accretion disk, it is logical to assume that they had nearly the same set of starter components: silicates, oxygen, carbon dioxide, nitrogen, and so on. When the planets first solidified, the sun was approximately 30% less intense than it is today. This difference would have kept the surface temperature on Venus below the boiling point of water. On both Venus and Earth, the water cycle of rain-evaporation-rain would have begun.

Earth and Venus have roughly the same amount of carbon dioxide (CO_2), but on Earth, most of the carbon dioxide is trapped in rocks by a process called chemical weathering: Liquid water reacts with carbon dioxide to form solid carbonates. This process also may have been occurring on Venus, but as the sun's energy output increased, the temperature of Venus gradually climbed above the boiling point for water. At this point, whenever carbon dioxide was exhaled into the atmosphere by volcanoes or some other geologic process, there was no longer any liquid water present to perform the chemical weathering process: Carbon dioxide levels in the Venusian atmosphere increased. Just like Earth's greenhouse effect, heat energy from the sun is absorbed by the Venusian surface and reradiated as long-wave radiation. The increased carbon dioxide levels in the Venusian atmosphere increase the ability of the atmosphere to reflect that long-wave radiation back toward the surface. Venus is a greenhouse that has gotten horribly out of control.

Mars, which is 10% of the mass of Earth, formed an orbit about 152% the radius of Earth's orbit. As would be expected, the planet is colder and has a weaker gravitational field than that of Earth. Mars's weak gravity allows some of the lighter, more energetic elements such as nitrogen (N_2) to escape into space. This process has been a gradual one, however, as the cooler Martian temperatures have not imparted much heat energy to the remaining elements. The result is that Mars, rich in carbon dioxide gases that compose 95% of its atmosphere, also retains respectable portions of nitrogen (2.7%) and oxygen (0.13%) with a trace of water vapor (0.03%). The average surface atmospheric pressure is quite low, however—0.008 atms—and the average surface temperature is –58° C (–73° F).

At one point in Mars's not-too-distant past, liquid water was clearly abundant. Visual evidence of ancient river beds, flood plains, lakes, and seas is apparent in nearly every frame of NASA-obtained surface imagery. It is believed that a large portion of this ancient water supply still exists somewhere on the planet, buried underneath the soil in a layer of permafrost or frozen into the part water ice, part carbon dioxide ice in the poles. Clouds can still be seen forming and moving across the Martian surface; seasonal temperature changes bring a hoarfrost to the landscape; and early morning radiation mist is apparent just after the Martian dawn.

The contradictory state of a frozen planet and low atmospheric pressure with clear signs of all three states of water existing has lead to the question: Is today's Mars a dying planet taking its last breath of life, or is it merely in a state of hibernation, waiting for some large-scale planetary Martian cycle (similar to Earth's ice ages) to retreat?

Comparison of Atmospheric Strata between Five Solar System Bodies

Although they were all born under the same star, the atmospheres of the planets and satellites that inhabit the solar system vary wildly in composition, density, temperature, structure, and pressure. This chart compares the atmospheric strata of three terrestrial planets, one gas giant, and one satellite of a gas giant.

The structure of Venus's atmosphere is heavily stratified, but all of the strata can be classified into three distinct layers. The *lower atmosphere* extends from the surface to about 50 kilometers in altitude. The air in the lower atmosphere is clear until about 30 kilometers above the surface, at which point a 20-kilometer layer of aerosol consisting of large particles, possibly free floating sulfur, begins. The *cloud deck* runs from 50 kilometers to 70 kilometers and consists primarily of thick clouds formed from sulfuric acid. The *upper atmosphere* runs from 70 kilometers on up, where sulfuric acid is still found, but in an aqueous solution. Because Venus has no substantial magnetic field, particles from the sun directly contact the upper atmosphere, and ionize a significant portion of it.

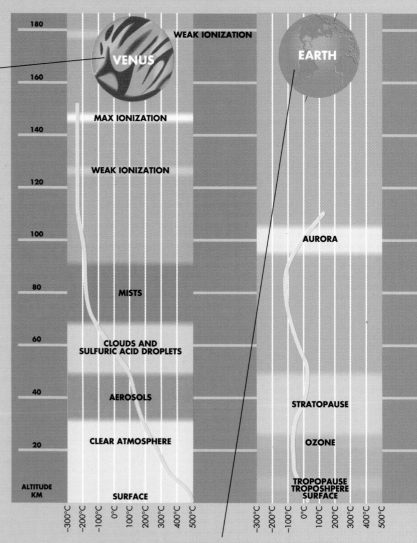

The strata of Earth's atmosphere have been well documented elsewhere. The main constituents are oxygen and nitrogen. In the lower altitudes, temperature decreases with altitude as the atmosphere rarefies. However, beyond the ozone layer, the temperature of the atmosphere once again begins to rise due to reradiated heat energy from the ozone's absorption of ultraviolet radiation from the sun.

The scales of these comparison charts are too shallow to present the models of Jupiter's atmospheres all the way down to its core—the planet is simply too large. Cloud structures deep within Jupiter's massive atmosphere are distinctly colored in each atmospheric stratum. The wispy, ethereal cirrus clouds of the troposphere are white and consist of ammonia-ice crystals at a temperature of about –123° C. The two cloud decks that give Jupiter some of its characteristic riot of colors are the reddish-brown, or ruddy, clouds that begin at about 120 kilometers from the top of the atmosphere. These clouds appear to be composed of hydrogen sulfide (H_2S) and nitrogen. Below these ruddy clouds are a deck of clouds that are brown in complexion, and appear to be composed of mostly water (H_2O) and some organic chemical compounds. The temperature at this level is warm enough (0° C) for water to exist at this state. Keep in mind that the atmosphere of Jupiter continues downward from this spot for more than 50,000 kilometers, the temperatures soar to over 20,000° C, and the atmospheric pressure increases to a mind-boggling 45 million atms.

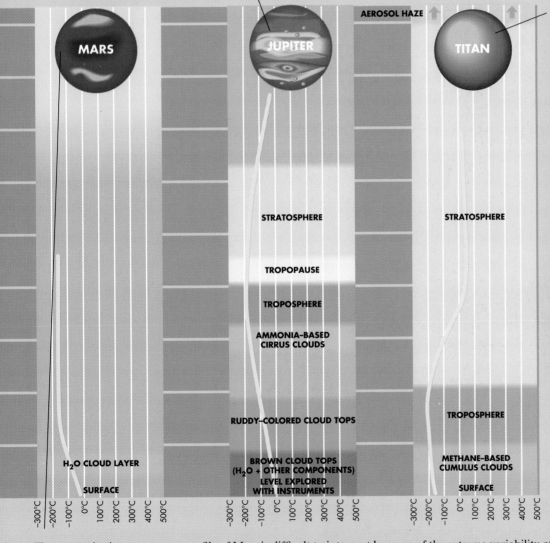

Titan is the sixth moon of Saturn, and more closely resembles a terrestrial planet than a natural satellite of another planet. Although it was discovered in 1655 by Christian Huygens, humans could only guess at its composition because of its extreme distance from Earth. Voyager 1 in 1980 and Voyager 2 in 1981 made flybys of this amazing satellite on their way through the Saturnian system. The images and spectroscopic analysis that came back from these spacecraft indicate that the atmospheric content of Titan may be rich in methane and, through photodissociation, it would allow the formation of hydrocarbons and other fundamental compounds of organic chemistry. Titan has been likened to a primordial Earth just prior to the creation of organic compounds. The best models to date indicate that frozen and liquid methane dominate the dynamics of Titan's atmosphere in a manner similar to the way water vapor dominates Earth's atmospheric dynamics.

The atmospheric temperature profile of Mars is difficult to interpret because of the extreme variability of the Martian atmosphere. In any given location near the Martian equator, for instance, the yearly seasonal cycle can vary the surface temperature anywhere from –100° C to 0° C. The Martian atmospheric temperature tends to drop with increased altitude, and does not deviate greatly from this linear course. The reason is that the Martian atmosphere does not contain layers that absorb solar radiation as do the atmospheres of Venus and Earth, so there is little chance for reradiation of energy at higher altitudes. Mars does not have a protective layer of ozone like Earth has, because the solar radiation breaks the carbon dioxide and water vapor into carbon monoxide (CO), atomic oxygen (O), the radical OH, and hydrogen (H), in a process called photodissociation. These four products of photodissociation interact in a way that retards the development of ozone.

Weather on the Final Frontier

VENUS IS A SLOW turner. It takes nearly 243 earth days for Venus to rotate once on its axis. This slow rotation is part of the reason the magnetic field on Venus is negligible. Combining the slow rotation of Venus with its thick atmosphere, astronomers were convinced that the winds on Venus were sluggish. When the Pioneer Venus spacecraft arrived for its 14-year tour of duty, however, that view changed. It was discovered that all altitude levels of the Venusian atmosphere *superrotate*, or travel faster than the surface rotates. (On Earth, only winds aloft superrotate.) At the high altitudes on Venus, the winds aloft are in excess of 100 meters per second, or 224 miles per hour.

Winds on other planets are powered in much the same way as they are here on Earth: Unequal heating between the lower latitudes and the upper latitudes creates pressure differences that cause the winds to flow. A complete flow pattern from one latitude to another constitutes a cell. Planetary rotation adds to the complexity of the cells' circulation by introducing the Coriolis effect: North-south winds are deflected to east-west directions, and these new deflected winds are called zonal winds. (In fact, all east-west winds are zonal.) On Earth, zonal winds at the middle latitudes move much more slowly than the planet rotates, so the winds blow eastward. On Venus, however, the atmosphere at all latitudes superrotate, so all winds blow westward.

Mars's atmosphere, for all its high carbon dioxide composition and low pressure, still surprises scientists by exhibiting weather that is remarkably familiar. As early as the nineteenth century, astronomers noticed that Mars was broken into dark and light patches. As the Martian year wore on, the dark patches would show seasonable variability and alternately grow and shrink. The logical conclusion was that the dark patches were some form of vegetation responding to the warmer Martian summers. The debate over Martian vegetation continued until 1964 when Mariner 4 flew by Mars and found no evidence of vegetation. What were the dark patches? Dust.

In 1971, the Soviet Mars 3 entered the thin Martian atmosphere on schedule, touched the ground, and promptly disappeared. A few years later, the American Mariner 9 went into orbit around the Red Planet. There it saw what Mars 3 experienced, and what was the source of the seasonal changes viewable from Earth: Mars was in the throes of a planetary dust storm. Seasonal variations in the heating of the upper and lower latitudes had generated winds of 140 meters per second, or 0.087 miles per second; nearly half the speed that sound travels on Mars. (Due to the low atmospheric density of Mars, such winds would only be able to lift fine silt and dust.) The seasonal melting and refreezing of the Martian polar caps completed the picture: Seasonal roving dust storms and growing and shrinking polar ice looked to Earth-bound observers like vegetable growth causing seasonal variability in the appearance of the Martian disk.

Because of the thin atmosphere and low water content, Mars is not subjected to storm systems of the same variety as those on Earth, but some parallels can be found. Mars's atmosphere can support atmospheric vortices that are analogous to vortices found on Earth. Martian dust devils, for instance, have been imaged by the U.S. Viking orbiters, and it is suspected that their formation is similar to that of their terrene cousins. Vortices of greater intensity may also exist in the Martian environment.

In 1987, researcher John Grant at Brown University's Department of Geological Sciences may have found evidence of Martian atmospheric vortices that are the equivalent of Earth's tornadoes. Dark streak patterns in the Martian soil were imaged first by Mariner 9, and then by both Viking I and Viking II orbiters. Prior to the Viking missions, the dark streaks, or *lineations*, were hypothesized to be a form of linear sand dune, but this explanation does not fit the evidence provided by Viking. The lineations are seasonal, appearing on the orbiter images near the end of the martian summer. Although they were noted across the planet, the highest density of lineations was noted in the mid-latitude regions. The local topography of Mars appears to have had no effect in either the deviation or creation of these streaks; they regularly cross over crater rims and drop down to the crater floors with no change in their trajectory.

These pieces of evidence correspond with creation times, locations, and behavior of terrene tornadoes: appearing late in the summer when ground heat is at its maximum, and concentrating in the mid-latitude regions of the planet. Evidence such as this gives rise to the idea that these lineations are paths from intense Martian wind vortices, similar to tornado destruction paths on Earth. How intense are these vortices? The exact vortex wind velocity is not known, but it is believed that the dark appearance of the lineations is caused by overturning of the martian soil. The thin atmosphere of Mars requires an inordinately strong wind to move material as heavy as soil, and the images of the Martian dust devils show that they are not intense enough to leave the lineation patterns in their wake. The question of Martian tornadoes will have to wait until future missions to the Red Planet are underway.

One of the many surprises of the U.S. Voyager missions was the Saturnian satellite Titan. Covered in an icy layer of smoglike haze, Titan's molecular nitrogen-rich atmosphere is home to conditions that one would not expect to find so far from the sun.

Voyager's infrared spectrometers revealed that, although its surface is obscured by haze, Titan has a surprisingly warm surface temperature of –178° C (–288° F). Measurements of the *attenuation of signal*, the gradual weakening of signal strength, of the Voyager transmission as Titan passed between Earth and the spacecraft revealed a surface pressure of 1.6 atmospheres (atms).

Titan has more free nitrogen in its atmosphere than any other planetary body in the solar system besides Earth. The most active gas in its atmosphere is methane, which the sun photodissociates into hydrogen molecules and methane radicals. These three constituents (hydrogen, methane, and nitrogen) combine to form complex hydrocarbons such as ethane, ethylene, and acetylene. These hydrocarbons, as well as a few other molecules, condense out into a fine mist of particulate matter, or aerosol, at the higher, colder altitudes, and constitute the haze surrounding Titan. This haze performs the same function that ozone does on Earth: to absorb and scatter ultraviolet sunlight.

The photodissociation of molecular nitrogen forms nitrogen atoms, which combine with some of the other constituents to form hydrogen cyanide. As lethal as hydrogen cyanide sounds, it is one of the key building blocks in organic chemistry. More than a few atmospheric scientists have noted that the hydrocarbon-rich atmosphere of Titan is probably quite similar to the early atmosphere of the infant Earth.

Although the surface conditions on Titan cannot be studied without sending a lander to the surface (pending funding, NASA plans on such a mission, to be called Cassini), the atmospheric conditions near the surface of the planet can be inferred from the evidence that has been obtained so far. The temperature at the surface, combined with the evidence of abundant methane in the atmosphere, suggests that liquid methane exists on the surface of Titan. The process of convection would be effective in the thicker, warmer atmosphere within 30 kilometers of the surface. These two assertions lead to the conjecture that clouds of methane vapor appear in the Titanian troposphere.

Even the most conservative models for the Titanian meteorology indicate that the weather of Titan is analogous to the weather of Earth, except that liquid methane, not liquid water, is the principle controlling factor. In a bizarre twist on the Earth's water cycle, billowy cumulonimbus clouds of methane are steered through the skies of Titan by pressure imbalances in the atmosphere. These methane clouds are capable of producing liquid methane precipitation that adds to the liquid methane table beneath the surface of the planet. Eventually, the liquid methane finds its way back into the clouds via the processes of convection and dynamic lifting. If the surface topology of Titan is sufficient to allow methane-laden air to rise to a suitable condensation layer, orographic lifting will provide the basis for a third cloud-making process.

Atmospheric Events on Other Terrestrial Planets

To the naked eye, or to a visible-light camera, all that can be seen of Venus is the featureless, dull white of the planet's cloud tops. The Pioneer Venus spacecraft, however, was capable of imaging the planet with an ultraviolet filter: A definite pattern emerged. This chevron pattern in the cloud tops was originally believed to be a wake caused by the atmosphere blowing over a towering topographic feature on the planet's surface. In reality, however, the pattern is caused by the superrotation of the Venusian atmosphere.

Earth's atmosphere is broken up into six distinct circulation cells, caused by uneven heating across the planet's surface combined with the rapid rotation of the earth. In the mid-latitudes on Earth, the planet rotates faster than do the surface winds, giving way to eastward winds in those latitudes. On Venus, however, there are only two circulation cells: the North Hadley and the South Hadley. Unlike on Earth, all latitudes on Venus superrotate. The relative wind velocities between the ground and the air are lower at the lower latitudes, so the winds at the lower latitudes lag behind those at higher latitudes, resulting in the chevron pattern. No one knows why Venus's atmosphere superrotates, but it may have something to do with Venus's slow rotational velocity and its distance from the sun.

Venus

COOLER, HIGH PRESSURE

HOTTER, LOW PRESSURE

RELATIVE WIND VELOCITY

PLANETARY ROTATION

PLANETARY ROTATION

RELATIVE WIND VELOCITY

INTENSE SUNLIGHT

SLOW PLANETARY ROTATION

The Mariner and Viking spacecrafts photographed what appears to be wind vortex tracks on the surface of Mars. This image from the U.S. orbiter Viking I shows the faint vortex trails crossing geographic features on the surface: crater rims, crater floors, and surface gorges. This behavior is consistent with terrestrial wind vortex paths.

Mars

On Mars, as on Earth, temperatures in the late summer result in an unstable air situation. Packets of warm air rise through the colder air above them. There is very little water vapor in the atmosphere of Mars, unlike on Earth. Cloud formation does take place, however, and many images exist of Martian clouds being formed via orographic lifting.

Due to forces not quite understood, a horizontal wind vortex, similar in structure to the beginning stages of a terrestrial mesocyclone, forms over the surface. The formation of this horizontal wind vortex may be related to a cold front that has moved into the region of instability.

As in tornadogenesis on Earth, the rising warm air packets carry a portion of the horizontal vortex into the higher altitudes, where they encounter winds aloft.

A portion of the horizontal vortex becomes nearly perpendicular to the ground, and a vertical vortex is born. It is important to remember that the small amounts of water vapor make this a clear air phenomenon, unlike tornadoes on Earth. In addition, the thin Martian atmosphere makes it difficult for the vortex to have enough intensity to carry debris very high into its funnel.

Capturing an image of a strong Martian wind vortex will be very difficult, as the two primary factors that make a tornado on Earth visible are the condensation of water vapor and the transport of ground debris aloft.

HUMAN ACTIVITY AND THE ATMOSPHERE

CONTENTS

BASED ON REPORTS in the media, humanity is on the verge of being plunged into an ecological disaster of biblical proportions. The United States seemed to claim more than its fair share of meteorological incidents in recent times: 1993 and 1994 have given us earthquakes in Southern California, record floods along the Mississippi River, the Blizzard of '93, and record-breaking snowfall along the East Coast in 1993–1994. What is happening? Is the weather actually changing, and does the presence of human beings have anything to do with it?

This deceptively simple question is difficult to answer. The answer could easily be yes—humans do contribute to the changing weather patterns. There are now over 5 billion human beings living on the face of the earth, and over half of that number live in industrialized countries. The residents of these countries contribute to the modification of the atmosphere's chemical content through waste byproducts, and they contribute to the atmosphere's heat content by generating heat through industrialized activities. The percentage of the global population that does not live in industrialized countries also contributes to atmospheric modification. The depletion of the world's forests, for instance, is in part due to the collection of firewood and to slash-and-burn agriculture. The removal of the forests greatly alters the oxygen–carbon dioxide balance in the earth's atmosphere.

Another answer to the question "Is the world's weather changing?" would be: No one is sure. To be certain, the 1993–1994 winter season hit new records for snowfall and temperature drops, but what does that mean? The National Weather Service has not been around that long, and daily weather reports have only been gathering information since 1849 and then from only 200 sites. Reasonable weather records in the United States go back only about 90 years. In most other countries, they do not even go back that far. That our winters have gotten colder than any winter on record only means that it's the coldest it has been in roughly 90 years; not a long period of time, given the age of Earth. In fact, paleoclimatological records indicate the opposite: We are currently in one of the warmer periods in Earth's history. It is nearly impossible to detect changes in global climatological trends based on 90 years' worth of temperature recordings.

So, the answer is not so simple. It is nearly impossible to dismiss the deleterious effects of 5 billion humans swarming over the surface of the earth, but it's just as difficult to connect the interference by humans with changes in Earth's weather based on a scant 90 years of temperature profiles. However, as technology improves, new instrumentation allows us to see our planet in a different way. We can now reliably monitor our atmosphere's carbon dioxide content, measure the thickness of the ozone layer, and collect and record a hundred other pieces of data that we never had access to before.

Through the careful, concise analysis of this data, we may be able to detect changes and alterations in Earth's climatological behavior. Computer models can be provided with more accurate information in greater quantities with which to project trends. Still, all of this may not be enough: Earth's weather machine is a complex device, and there might be too many variables to possibly decipher them all. Still, some pieces of evidence are hard to dismiss. On top of Mauna Loa is a carbon dioxide monitoring facility. An analysis of the data obtained from this station shows a yearly increase in the carbon dioxide content of the atmosphere. Furthermore, the graph of the carbon dioxide increase nearly parallels the increase in fuel consumption around the world—there is even a dip in the data where the fuel crisis of the 1970s occurred.

For the first time in history, human beings are able to keep accurate records of the planet's environment. What we do with that data is the gauge by which we will be judged by other generations.

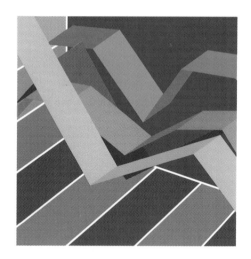

CHAPTER 20

Are the Earth's Weather Patterns Changing?

THIS IS NOT the same question as "Is the earth's climate changing?" Humans may be having an impact on our long-term global climate. Specific weather patterns, however, are a manifestation of all of the basic principles that this text has explored so far: interactions between the atmosphere and the ocean, the amount of sunlight absorbed by our planet, and so on. Although it can be argued that some of these principles—such as the amount of sunlight absorbed by our planet—have altered over the course of human existence, attaching blame to these factors for increased violent weather activity is a difficult task. In fact, there is significant evidence that violent weather activity has not increased at all.

How can we make this assertion? A glance at a newspaper or a television news broadcast will quickly have the viewer wondering if something serious has gone wrong with our planet. It seems that scarcely a day goes by that some area of the planet is not under siege by a hurricane, typhoon, blizzard, flood, or tornado. Try as we might, it is hard to recall a period in history when this many violent weather events occurred simultaneously. How can this be explained if there is not an increase in violent weather, or at least a change in the earth's weather patterns?

The increase is most likely not in the total number of violent weather events, but rather in the ability of humans to detect and report these events. The National Weather Service maintains over 300 weather reporting facilities in the United States, processing well over 20 million reports annually. In Kansas City, Missouri, the National Oceanographic and Atmospheric Association (NOAA) maintains the National Severe Storms Forecast Center, which is responsible for processing and releasing information regarding local severe storms to cities around the United States. In orbit around the planet are the Geostationary Operational Environmental Satellites, or GOES, which are also operated by the NOAA. The current GOES systems download visual and infrared satellite imagery every 40 minutes, and when it is required of them, they are capable of rapid transmissions of the same data every 20 minutes. All of these facilities became available within the past 50 years.

Do any of these modern sensors show significant change in global weather conditions? The debate is currently raging as to whether or not human activity is altering our long-term climate conditions, but there is very little evidence to support the assertion that short-term violent weather is on the increase. Even though we only have several decades of reliable data, mostly from the United States and Canada, examining this information begins to paint an interesting picture of what is occurring and why we perceive violent weather as a rapidly increasing problem.

The number of severe winters, storms, and scorching summers varies from year to year in a seemingly random pattern. This random pattern is referred to as noise in the data: random fluctuations in the data that, when taken as a whole, add up to nothing that is statistically significant. Humans, however, have interesting memory patterns: Over the long term, they seem to remember the worst events of a given period as being representative of that period. Over the short term, human beings tend to recall recent events as representative trends.

As a case in point, the late 1980s and early 1990s had some of the warmest winters on record. The snowfall for this period was less than two-thirds of the total snowfall during the period immediately following World War II. Media reports during the late '80s and early '90s were using this snowfall lull as evidence that the weather was being modified by human behavior and that winter conditions were becoming less harsh. Then came the winter of 1992–1993, the fourth coldest winter on record for the Northwestern United States. In the 1993–1994 winter season, the east coast of the United States received record-breaking snowfalls and a total of 17 winter storms. Gone were the speculations that the earth's weather was getting milder.

This human tendency to perceive current weather reports as long-term trends also applies to outbreaks of tornadoes, thunderstorms, floods, and hurricanes. All data collection techniques at our disposal indicate that the average number of yearly occurrences of these events is not on the increase, although specific storm population numbers fluctuate randomly year to year. Our ability to predict, detect, and track these events, however, is advancing at a phenomenal rate. As a result, the National Weather Service issues more warnings and alerts the media more often, so the perception is that these events are on the increase.

It is important at this point to recognize that modern weather detection and alert systems are normally only focused on the United States, Canada, Japan, and Europe. Other areas of the world are subject equally to the stress of violent weather, but little or no effort is put into the detection of these events, and few governments outside the industrialized world are prepared for getting information to their population or dealing with severe crisis conditions.

Data collection in other areas of the world is not as advanced as similar techniques in the United States and other technologically advanced countries. Global monitoring systems such as geostationary satellites do collect information from other areas of the planet, but ground stations, radar, and other local detection techniques are woefully inadequate outside the first world. This not only does a disservice to the residents of these countries, but it leaves gaps in the world weather database. Meteorologists working with global concerns must somehow infer information about the missing data, which could lead to overall flaws in global weather models.

A Sample of Severe Weather Activity from 1943 to 1992

Although paleoclimatologists collect weather and climate information from as far back as 1 million years ago, widespread reliable weather data (defined as data collected through direct measurement) is only available for the past 90 years, at most. The years from 1943 to 1992 were picked for this chart because of availability of information. The United States was chosen as the location, as this country is currently the world leader in atmospheric, meteorological, and climatological data collection.

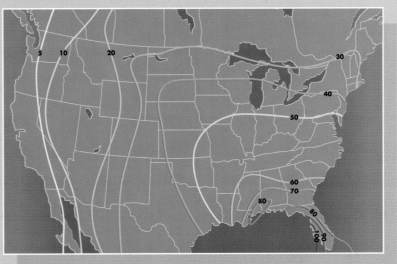

1 This contour map shows an approximation of the average yearly thunderstorm activity during the five-year period from 1980 to 1985 for the United States. In the period from 1943 to 1992, the positions of the contour lines are barely displaced from this average, and the average number of thunderstorms for each region only fluctuates by +/–3 storms.

2 The contours in this graph represent average tornado density values over the United States for the same 1980–1985 period. Surprisingly, although the total number of tornadoes in these regions can vary from the average by as many as +/– 8 tornadoes a year, the positions of the contour boundaries vary only slightly. In other words, although the number of tornadoes per region may increase or decrease on a yearly basis, the overall ratio of tornado densities across the country remains relatively unchanged.

3 This chart represents snowfall figures for 1943–1992. Although the lines only represent four U.S. cities, the placement of the cities across the country gives the reader some idea of the snowfall rates in different areas of the snow belt: Fairbanks, Alaska; Spokane, Washington; Fargo, North Dakota; and New York, New York. The lines represent deviations (in inches) from each area's total historical average snowfall. Although the snowfall rate does vary (considerably in the case of Washington state), there is no clear indication from this data that snowfall rates are either increasing or decreasing in these areas.

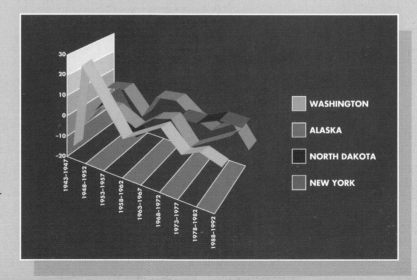

The Role of Life in the Climate Equation

BY CONSIDERING ONLY the mechanical aspects of chemical and physical processes when forming global climate models, we fail to take into account one of the primary forces influencing events on this planet: the role of life itself. Unlike any other planet of which we are aware, life swarms over the surface of the earth from pole to pole. The effect that life has had on this planet becomes apparent when studying other, lifeless planetary bodies in our solar system. On these other planets, only the mechanical processes of physics and chemistry combine to provide their climates and geology. Erosion processes on Mars, for instance, rely entirely on wind and possibly water: Mountains on Mars are enormous by Earth standards, and planetary dust storms are common. On Earth, however, the presence of plant life on an otherwise barren landscape prevents the erosion of topsoil, while the plants on the face of a mountain help break up the rock face to aid in wind erosion.

The interaction of plant and animal life with the global climate, and the effect this interaction has on the process of climate change and modification is only now beginning to be fully understood. Climate, which can be loosely defined in terms of the meteorologic conditions of temperature, precipitation, pressure, and so on, is very much dependent upon the chemical composition of the atmosphere. Different gases behave in different ways when exposed to the environmental conditions of Earth, such as the amount of energy Earth receives from the sun.

It is fairly clear from paleoclimatological studies that the current levels of oxygen, nitrogen, and carbon dioxide in the atmosphere were greatly influenced by the formation of life on this planet. It is when life first formed that oxygen and carbon dioxide production began in earnest. This process became self-regulating soon after plants began to photosynthesize; a process whereby plants use the energy from the sun to remove water and carbon dioxide from the air and transform it into sugars, which the plant uses, and oxygen, which is released back into the atmosphere as a byproduct. When the plants die, their bacterial decomposition releases the carbon dioxide back into the atmosphere. Carbon dioxide is also released into the atmosphere by the respiration of animals. Carbon dioxide is one of the *greenhouse gases*, a collection of atmospheric gases that conspire to keep a certain percentage of longwave radiation from escaping back into space. These gases keep the planet warm, which in turn allows more life to form and survive.

There is an important relationship at work here: Plants require carbon dioxide to live, which they obtain from the atmosphere. The atmosphere requires a certain level of carbon dioxide to maintain a temperature and climate that is also required by the plant to live. When the plant dies, it relinquishes carbon dioxide back into the atmosphere, helping to maintain the overall carbon dioxide balance which, in turn, helps maintain a certain climate condition. This mechanism of carbon dioxide production/protection is called biological feedback.

It is important to note that not everyone subscribes to this holistic view of the planet. Few deny that the process of biological feedback is occurring. What has been questioned, however, is whether biological feedback has a less significant impact on the constituency of the atmosphere, and therefore the nature of our global climate. The lessons of other planets not withstanding, some argue that the composition of the atmosphere is being maintained and regulated purely by the laws of physics and chemistry: The majority of carbon dioxide, it is claimed, is released into the atmosphere via volcanic emissions. The carbon dioxide gas is removed from the atmosphere by the process of chemical weathering: The carbon dioxide is literally washed out of the sky by the rain and is carried off into the water table, where it forms carbonates that will be belched back into the atmosphere by volcanic activity. Earth, it is claimed, would be habitable even if it were uninhabited.

In the early 1980s, biologist James Lovecock proposed that both of these mechanisms, biological feedback and pure geophysics, do not act independently, but in conjunction. The process of life itself, for example, aids the geophysical process of chemical weathering: Organisms help break up the rocks into soil, which increases rock surface area and allows for greater absorption of the carbon dioxide from the rain. In 1989, further research confirmed that, in fact, chemical weathering of carbon dioxide into rocks like basalt proceeds 1,000 times faster in the presence of microorganisms than it does when the rock is sterile.

In other examples, Lovecock points out that deep sea organisms absorb calcium carbonates and use them to form their protective shells. When these organisms die, their shells become part of the rock strata and the carbon dioxide reenters the system via geophysical processes. These examples of reciprocity between life, the atmosphere, the oceans, and the land are analogous to how various parts of an organism regulate that organism's life processes. This concept forms the core of an ecological view of the earth as a single, large, metabolizing entity. This entity has been given a name: *Gaia*, the Greek word for Earth.

By whatever mechanism or combination of mechanisms, the content of the atmosphere does appear to go through incremental changes in its content. The atmosphere of the present day is not the same as the atmosphere of a million years ago, which, in turn, is not the same as the atmosphere of a million years before then. All of this regulation, however, occurs over a long time scale. As one source of an atmospheric gas begins to increase, a mechanism develops either to remove that gas from the atmosphere or to adapt to the addition of the new atmospheric component.

The debate becomes heated when we add human beings to the equation. As of the time of this writing, the citizens of the earth total over 5.5 billion, and form the largest single constituent of multicelled animals outside of the insect family. Like every other organism on the planet, we add to the global atmospheric content simply through the process of breathing (carbon dioxide) and excreting (methane). Like every other organism, we generate heat with our bodies (500 British Thermal Units, or BTUs, per hour per person). Unlike every other organism, however, we consciously manipulate our environment to provide ourselves with energy. We burn wood and fossil fuels to stay warm, we cut down forests to make room for crops and farmland, and we build cities and factories. These environment-manipulating activities all produce chemical byproducts, or hamper natural atmospheric and geophysical regulating mechanisms. The scale at which these activities are occurring is beginning to cause measurable changes in the constituency of the atmosphere.

On the top of a mountain called Mauna Loa in Hawaii, a chemist named Charles Keeling established a carbon dioxide monitoring station in 1958. He chose Hawaii because of its location in the middle of the Pacific ocean, far from the hustle and bustle of most of the Western world. The east-to-west air currents would blow clean, unpolluted air over the mountaintop. In order for carbon dioxide levels to change at Mauna Loa, Keeling reasoned, the total global concentration of carbon dioxide would have to be altered. From Mauna Loa, Keeling believed he could monitor the entire planet's carbon dioxide level.

Regardless of what arguments can be made against Keeling's reasoning, the results from his monitoring station are astonishing. All paleoclimatological evidence points to the fact that prior to the industrialization of the Western world, the global atmospheric concentration of carbon dioxide hovered at around 275 parts per million (PPM), with a variation of +/– 10 PPM. The Mauna Loa station has been operating continuously since 1958. During the brief 36 years of its monitoring, Mauna Loa has shown a continuous increase in the levels of carbon dioxide. This steadily rising data curve is sometimes referred to as the Keeling Curve. The current atmospheric content, according to Mauna Loa, is now over 350 PPM.

Other atmospheric gases are also on the rise—chlorofluorocarbons, methane, and nitrous oxide, to name a few. What conclusions can be drawn from all of this? Perhaps none. The same logic applied to the question of increased violent weather activity could also be applied here: We have only been in the business of precise atmospheric monitoring for a relatively short period of time. Perhaps the paleoclimatological evidence is incorrect, and the earth periodically goes through fluctuations of carbon dioxide input into our atmosphere that have never been measured prior to the past 50 years. If this is the case, the Keeling Curve should not concern us.

If the earth has an infinite capacity to renew itself and maintain a balance of gases in its atmosphere, then localized environmental horror stories such as overpolluted cities or acid rain can be thought of as isolated incidents of little or no consequence to the rest of the planet. When one steps back and examines the earth as a whole, however, this possibility seems more and more remote. The earth is a finite vessel that contains a finite amount of chemical compounds maintained in a delicate balance by the forces of life, geology, and chemistry. It has an amazing ability to regulate its atmospheric equilibrium in response to gradual changes in global production or removal of constituent gases. Humans, however, have the ability to produce atmospheric gases or inhibit mechanisms that control atmospheric regulating on an enormous scale in a relatively short time frame. Can the earth's natural regulatory processes keep pace with human activity?

Carbon Dioxide Levels and the Human Factor

Direct measurements indicate that human activities are modifying the content of our atmospheric gases on a global scale. Greenhouse gases such as carbon dioxide, methane, and nitrous oxide appear to be on the increase. What this will mean to long-term climatological change is uncertain. This chart offers a recording of carbon dioxide levels in the atmosphere and relates the information to significant events in the industrial age.

Reliable methods of measuring this information have only come into being in the last 40 years or so. Information prior to the 1950s was obtained by paleoclimatological methods (gas bubbles trapped in arctic ice, for example) and, as such, may be unreliable.

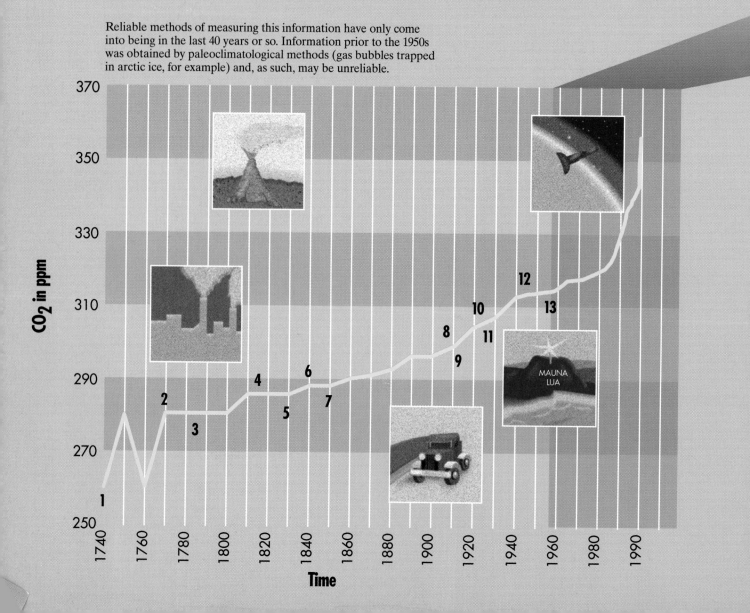

CO_2 in ppm

Time

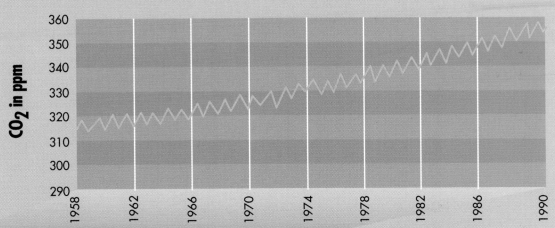

In 1958, a carbon dioxide–monitoring station was set up on Mauna Loa in Hawaii, and the first direct measurements of the carbon dioxide level in the atmosphere began. The cyclic fluctuations in this monthly average data are due to yearly decomposition and growth of vegetable matter, resulting in increased emissions of carbon dioxide in the autumn and winter in the Northern Hemisphere, and a similar, yet smaller, oscillation during the Southern Hemisphere's autumn and winter. The overall trend, however, shows a clear increase in carbon dioxide levels over the course of the nearly 40-year study.

1 1740   The process of smelting steel is improved to the point where mass production becomes possible.

2 1775   James Watt invents the steam engine.

3 1784   English ironmaster Henry Cort introduces the puddling process for the manufacture of wrought iron.

4 1815   A Volcanic eruption in Tambora, India kills 90,000 people. An unknown amount of carbon dioxide and particulate matter is released into the atmosphere.

5 1828   Construction completed on the *Baltimore–Ohio*, the first United States railroad built specifically for the transportation of freight and passengers. Other countries follow suit, and the age of intercontinental mass transit has begun.

6 1840   Mass production techniques improve to the point of allowing the distribution of artificial fertilizers on a large scale.

7 1850   The Little Ice Age ends around this time, and the first reliable temperature recordings begin in the United States.

8 1908   First commercial manufacture of Bakelite marks the beginning of the age of plastics. Plastic manufacture increases rapidly from this point.

9 1911   Charles Kettering develops the first practical electric starter for automobiles. This moves automobiles out of the toy-for-the-rich phase as mass production techniques bring the cost down to affordable levels for most Americans and Europeans.

10 1923   Mass steel production gets a large boost when John Tytus invents a way to produce a continuous strip of molten steel.

11 1927   The 15 millionth Model T Ford rolls off the assembly line.

12 1945   The first atomic bomb is detonated in Alamogordo, New Mexico. The atomic age begins.

13 1957   The USSR lauches Sputnik I and II. The space age begins.

CHAPTER 22

Global Warming: Myth or Reality?

AT THE CORE of the debate over human interference in the earth's global climate is whether or not the presence of human beings in the postindustrial age is contributing to an effect that has been dubbed *global warming*, the gradual increase in the earth's overall temperature. This debate is being waged on two fronts: one in the scientific circles and a second, more public front, in the media. Although both feed off each other (global climatologists enjoy increased funding when the media fuels the public debate, and the media sells more papers and airtime when the climatologists publish their reports), there are times when the climatological reports are misinterpreted by the media. This misinterpretation contributes to misinformation, which can lead to ill-informed responses by the public.

The general public commonly confuses the terms global warming and the greenhouse effect. Although connected, these two terms are not equivalent. The *greenhouse effect* refers to the physical process by which the presence of atmospheric gases allow the earth to maintain a higher equilibrium temperature than would otherwise occur in their absence. Global warming, in contrast, refers to a steady, long-term increase in this equilibrium temperature.

Incoming solar radiation is absorbed by the land and the oceans, and then reradiated at longer wavelengths. This longwave, infrared radiation would leak back into space were it not for the presence of the *greenhouse gases*: water vapor, carbon dioxide, methane, nitrous oxide, and ozone. Some of the greenhouse gases directly reflect the heat back to the surface; others absorb and reemit the heat to the earth's surface.

Fortunately, these gases are not perfectly efficient, so our atmospheric thermal blanket allows some of the heat energy to escape back into space. The result is that the planet is warmer due to the presence of these gases than it would be if they did not exist, but the inefficient insulation properties of the gases allow the earth's temperature to be in a life-tolerant range. If it were not for the greenhouse effect, life as we know it would never have arisen on earth; it would have been far too cold. Some estimates place the average temperature of the earth in the range of -25° F to -10° F if the gases did not exist.

Greenhouse gases were originally released into our atmosphere solely by a wide variety of natural geological and geochemical sources: volcanic activity, outgassing from rocks, and so on. When life first appeared on the planet, it greatly contributed to the greenhouse gases: Plants absorb carbon dioxide, which is released again when the plants die and rot. Animals inhale oxygen and metabolize it into carbon dioxide, which they then exhale, and dead animals release trapped gases such as methane when they decompose. Animal excretions, from bacterial decay to cow dung, are responsible for supplying huge amounts of methane to the atmosphere.

As we have observed, however, there is now a new source of these gases on the planet Earth: human activities in the postindustrial age. Data from the Mauna Loa station adds to the significant pool of mounting evidence concluding that carbon dioxide levels are up 50% from their preindustrial-age numbers. Increases in animal husbandry, fossil fuel recovery and burning, and landfills have raised the level of atmospheric methane (CH_4) to twice its preindustrial-age concentration. Nitrous oxide (N_2O) levels also seem be be increasing in the postindustrial age, albeit at a much slower rate, although the source of the increase has not been determined.

Based on these increases in greenhouse gas levels, the World Climate Conference declared in 1988 that planet Earth had a serious problem, and world governments had better start paying attention. This increase in global production of greenhouse gases, we were told, could cause the earth's greenhouse effect to become more efficient, which in turn might cause the global temperature average to rise to a level at which the global climate is significantly altered. The increase in greenhouse gases could lead to a *runaway greenhouse effect*, which would cause an overall trend of global warming.

Around this time, funding was increased significantly for research into the consequences of the human production of greenhouse gases. Computer models were devised, polar ice cap core samples were taken, satellites began archiving infrared temperature data to monitor trends in the global temperature, and archives were made of global cloud coverage to determine if there was a trend toward increasing cloud cover, which might be a sign of increased water vapor. Computer models churned and produced numbers indicating that the overall global temperature of the earth from 1979 to 1993 should have increased by $0.29°$ C ($0.65°$ F). If production of greenhouse gases is not curbed, the computer models indicate that by two decades into the next century, the global temperature will have increased by $2.8°$ C to $5.6°$ C ($5°$ F to $10°$ F).

However, findings that are being released now paint a different picture than what is depicted in the computer models. Monitoring of global temperatures by infrared satellite, for instance, have shown an increase of only $0.08°$ C ($0.16°$ F) in the temperature average since 1979. In addition, although the CO_2 levels are clearly rising, they are not rising as fast as would be expected, based on the carbon dioxide output of cars, industry, and fossil fuel consumption. Some natural factor in the earth's environment is removing some of the CO_2 from the system. So, were the climatologists wrong? Did we realize, on the eve of world government agreements to roll the production of greenhouse gases back to 1990 levels, that we may have been overreacting?

The answers are as difficult as the questions. As this text has tried to stress, the atmosphere of the earth, and its interaction with the planet and life on the planet, is extremely complex. The ability of humans to examine and digest all of the data relating to that interaction, although increasing at an exponential rate, is still woefully inadequate to the task. The computer predictions that temperatures would increase because of increased availability of greenhouse gases were only as correct as the information fed into the computer models: Clearly, other processes unknown to the models are at work.

So the computer models were too aggressive with their numbers; still, the actual, measured temperature values do show an increase since 1979. Is this proof that the increase in greenhouse gases is causing global warming, albeit at a slower pace? Maybe not: There are precedents for this rise in temperature. Recall that our current global temperature is not the warmest it has ever been in the history of planet Earth. Our current geologic age is called the Holocene period. According to paleoclimatological records, the global temperature average was warmer than it is today five times during the Holocene. The most recent warm period was A.D. 1000 to around A.D. 1450, and is referred to as the medieval warm period. Clearly, there were too few humans and too little industry present over those 450 years for human activity to have been responsible. Variations in the sun's energy output and periodic volcanic eruptions might be enough to explain short-term, planetary temperature fluctuations.

Taking these arguments at face value, however, may cause the pendulum of opinion to swing too far in the other direction. Certainly the computer models depicting atmospheric temperature increases were too liberal: The temperature has not increased in step with the models. However, estimates in the other direction may prove to be too conservative: By ignoring the problem, we may make it worse. So where does this all leave us?

The facts are that direct measurements of the earth's atmospheric content indicate that carbon dioxide, methane, water vapor, and nitrous oxide are all on the rise. The beginning of the upward trend in the level of these gases corresponds to the beginning of the industrial revolution. Although treaties were signed at the 1992 Earth Summit to roll back CO_2 emissions to 1990 levels, there are no specific plans to do so by any government. At the time of this writing, the administration of current United States president Bill Clinton has called for a series of volunteer actions by American industry to help comply with the emission rollbacks. Even if American industry carries out the administration's requests, it would still leave the United States with an annual CO_2 output 40 million tons over the 1990 emissions levels.

The increase in carbon dioxide in the atmosphere has not kept pace with the amount of CO_2 that humans daily pump into the atmosphere. Although at first glance this may seem like good news, no one is exactly sure where the extra CO_2 is going. There is some evidence that deciduous forests absorb more of the gas than was originally thought, but it is unclear why they are performing this function, since they do not need those levels of CO_2 to live. Also, what is the capacity of these forests to absorb CO_2? Can they keep pace with human production forever?

The earth has been able to regulate its naturally occurring greenhouse gases to levels that are within the acceptable range for carbon-based life. This regulation began far back in the earth's history, after the planet cooled from its initial formation. When plant and animal life arrived on the scene, the earth's atmosphere had to cope with an increase in greenhouse gases. Eventually, the atmospheric system struck a new equilibrium, and the biosphere continued its self-regulatory behavior. Now, once again, the earth is faced with a new source of input for these gases. Eventually, a new equilibrium will be reached, because that is the way of nature. However, by the time the new self-regulation takes place, it may be too late for the current residents.

Earth's Normal Greenhouse Effect

Although often confused with global warming, the earth's greenhouse effect is a natural consequence of the chemical makeup of the atmosphere. If it were not for the insulating properties of the greenhouse effect, life as we know it could not exist on the earth: It would be too cold. Today, greenhouse gas (carbon dioxide, methane, nitrous oxide, water vapor, and ozone) concentrations are on the rise. Although some speculate that unbalancing the current concentrations of greenhouse gases could lead to global warming, there is not enough information to say with any certainty what will happen.

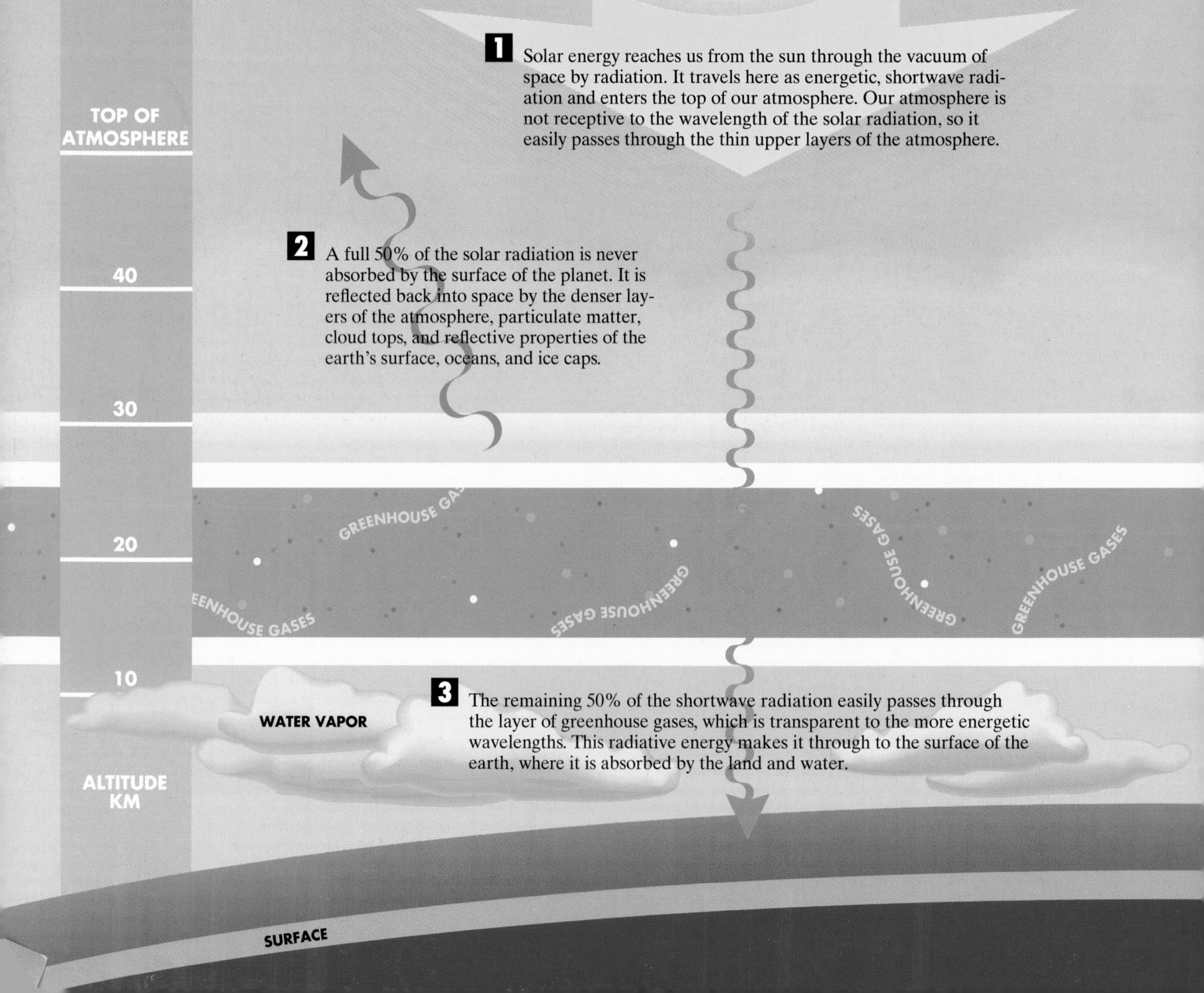

1 Solar energy reaches us from the sun through the vacuum of space by radiation. It travels here as energetic, shortwave radiation and enters the top of our atmosphere. Our atmosphere is not receptive to the wavelength of the solar radiation, so it easily passes through the thin upper layers of the atmosphere.

TOP OF ATMOSPHERE

2 A full 50% of the solar radiation is never absorbed by the surface of the planet. It is reflected back into space by the denser layers of the atmosphere, particulate matter, cloud tops, and reflective properties of the earth's surface, oceans, and ice caps.

40

30

GREENHOUSE GASES

20

GREENHOUSE GASES

10

WATER VAPOR

3 The remaining 50% of the shortwave radiation easily passes through the layer of greenhouse gases, which is transparent to the more energetic wavelengths. This radiative energy makes it through to the surface of the earth, where it is absorbed by the land and water.

ALTITUDE KM

SURFACE

6 Although most of the longwave radiation is prevented from leaving by the greenhouse gases, ultimately 12% of the emission passes through the gases and escapes into space.

7 The longwave radiation redirected back to the earth by the greenhouse gases is once again absorbed by the land and water at the surface of the earth. The cycle of reemission and reflection is repeated with the original packet of energy diminishing by 12% each time until all of it finally escapes into space.

GREENHOUSE GASES

GREENHOUSE GASES

GREENHOUSE GASES

GREENHOUSE GASES

GREENHOUSE GASES

GREENHOUSE GASES

4 The land and water act as heat sinks, storing the energy received from the sun via shortwave radiation. This energy is then reemitted as less energetic, long-wave, infrared radiation headed back toward space.

5 When the longwave radiation reaches the region of the greenhouse gases, most of it is either immediately reflected back toward the earth or absorbed and reemitted. The escape of heat from the planet is significantly reduced.

Venus's Greenhouse Effect

Like Earth's atmosphere, Venus's atmosphere has a greenhouse-effect mechanism that heats the planet. Unlike Earth, Venus has an extremely powerful greenhouse effect, caused by an overabundance of carbon dioxide. The carbon dioxide reacts with the sulfuric rocks on the surface to form an additional greenhouse gas that Earth does not possess in abundance: sulfur dioxide. The result of this intense greenhouse effect is soaring temperatures and bone-crushing atmospheric pressure.

1 Being closer to the sun than Earth, Venus has more incoming solar radiation.

3 Because Venus has 100% cloud cover all of the time (as opposed to Earth's estimated 50% cloud cover), the upper level of haze and the cloud tops conspire to reflect nearly 80% of the incoming radiation back into space. Of the remaining 20%, an additional 10% is absorbed by the upper atmosphere and reemitted back into space.

2 Like on Earth, the energetic, shortwave radiation penetrates Venus's upper atmosphere easily.

SULFURIC ACID HAZE

UPPER CLOUD DECK

MIDDLE CLOUD DECK

LOWER CLOUD DECK

4 The remaining 10% of the solar radiation penetrates the Venusian atmosphere to reach the surface, where it is absorbed by the rock and soil.

SURFACE

6 Unlike on Earth, where a full 12% of the longwave radiation escapes the notice of the greenhouse gas layer, hardly any of this radiation escapes through the greenhouse gas layer on Venus. However, once the tiny value of this escaping energy is added to the energy from the original shortwave radiation initially scattered back into space, most of the energy received from the sun is reemitted into space by Venus.

80

60

5 In a process similar to what happens on Earth, the feeble solar energy that makes it to the surface to be absorbed is reemitted as less energetic, longwave infrared radiation.

40

7 The longwave radiation redirected to the surface of Venus by the greenhouse gases is once again absorbed by the land and water at the surface. This energy is reemitted and once again most is reflected back by the Venusian greenhouse gases. The planet has reached its energy balance, and its surface temperature is 450° C (842° F).

20

ALTITUDE KM

Earth's Greenhouse Gas Cycle

It is difficult to express this information on a cycle chart, because we do not have all of the pieces in place. The exact quantities of output and total input of each of the sources and sinks for the gases are unknown. Nonetheless, we can get an idealized view of how all the earth's components interact to keep our planet at its current global temperature.

Human activity   Although humans have contributed to the greenhouse gases for millions of years in the same fashion as other animals, only in the last 150 years have they been able to produce greenhouse gases as a byproduct of their industrial processes. Through factories, industrial and energy plants, automobiles, planes, and other sources, humanity is dumping tens of millions of tons of carbon dioxide, methane, sulfur, and water vapor into the atmosphere at an ever-quickening rate. The amount will likely increase as more and more countries become industrialized.

Geologic processes   Vast quantities of carbon dioxide are released via periodic volcanic eruptions. Between 20 and 30 volcanic eruptions occur each year, spewing millions of tons of CO_2 into the atmosphere.

Life   By far the single largest contributing factor to carbon dioxide, methane, and other constituent greenhouse gas levels are the plants and animals that inhabit the planet. Animals and plants metabolize oxygen and water vapor and turn it into carbon dioxide. When plants die, the carbon dioxide they absorb during their lifetime is released during the decomposition process. Likewise, bacteria aiding the decomposition of dead animals release vast quantities of methane as a byproduct. Living things contribute hundreds of millions of tons of greenhouse gases to the atmosphere annually.

Unknown   There is still a lot contributing to the cycle that we do not yet understand. For example, one of the greenhouse gases, nitrous oxide (N_2O), has been steadily increasing over the past 150 years. This seems to coincide with the postindustrial age, but no one is certain how the gas is being produced.

Agriculture   Many forms of agriculture yield surprising amounts of constituent greenhouse gases. Rice paddies feed well over half of the world population, and they also produce vast quantities of methane. (The methane is not produced by the rice, but rather by bacteria feeding on the decomposing roots of the rice plant.) Countries that raise cows and other herd animals also contribute to the overall atmospheric methane contribution through the dung produced by these animals.

Chemical weathering   Through the process of chemical weathering, carbon dioxide is removed from the atmosphere and transported to the land and the oceans. The CO_2 reacts with the water to form solid carbonates which are, in turn, trapped in rocks. The trapped CO_2 will later be released through geologic processes.

Plant metabolism   Plants use energy from the sun to transform water vapor and carbon dioxide in the atmosphere into sugars that they then metabolize, and oxygen that they exhale. New information suggests that the deciduous forests of the northern regions of North America, Europe, and Asia may actually be absorbing more carbon dioxide than was previously believed. This may account for the lower observed levels of carbon dioxide than was predicted.

Unknown   Other processes are at work on our planet removing excess amounts of greenhouse gases, or the observed levels of these gases would be higher than they are now based on known gas inputs. This is clearly a signal that we do not understand all of the forces at work. The biggest question mark, however, is whether all of these processes that remove greenhouse gases are capable of keeping pace with increased human activity.

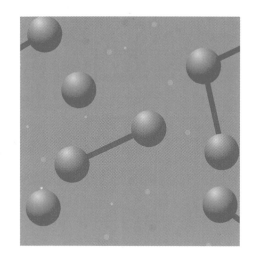

Nimbus 7 and the Ozone Controversy

N 1978, NASA launched the Nimbus 7 satellite. The satellite was designed to circle the earth in a *polar orbit,* which means that the satellite trajectory runs in a circle, taking it over both the North and South Poles. The majority of earth observation, weather, and telecommunications satellites circle the earth in an *equatorial orbit,* where the spacecraft's trajectory encircles the equator of the earth. Polar orbit satellites are more difficult to place into position, because they require special midflight maneuverings that equatorial orbit satellites do not. The advantage of launching earth observation satellites into polar orbits, however, comes into play once the orbit is established. As the satellite orbits, the earth rotates out from underneath the spacecraft, allowing complete coverage of the surface of the entire planet with a minimal amount of work.

Nimbus 7 was equipped with *TOMS*, or *total ozone mapping spectrometer*, an instrument intended to monitor the ozone (O_3) content of the earth's atmosphere continuously during a 24-hour period. The method for doing this turned out to be rather simple: Ozone is formed when ultraviolet radiation from the sun interacts with oxygen (O_2) molecules in the upper atmosphere. The ultraviolet light splits the oxygen into separate oxygen atoms (O). These free-floating oxygen atoms then recombine with oxygen molecules to form the ozone ($O + O_2 = O_3$). The resultant molecule is impervious to ultraviolet radiation; O_3 is the earth's protection against life-threatening ultraviolet radiation from the sun. The TOMS instrument simply measured the total amount of ultraviolet sunlight scattered by the atmosphere over which the satellite was passing.

The thickness of the atmospheric ozone layers recorded by TOMS is measured in *Dobson units,* or *DU*. The Dobson unit scale is arranged so that the measured thickness of the ozone layer is represented as a function of the thickness of pure ozone gas at normal sea level temperature and pressure conditions. The Dobson scale is not linear, but it works out that 300 DU would equal 3 millimeters of pure ozone gas at sea level.

In the last few years of the 1980s, when all of the information collected from TOMS began to be looked at as a function of time, a very disturbing pattern emerged. Data collected from TOMS in 1979 showed ozone concentrations around the world that appeared to be what meteorologists and atmospheric scientists were expecting: some seasonal variations, with higher concentrations around the tropics than at the poles. It is believed that these disparities in ozone coverage are due to the behavior of gas under the influence of the spinning earth.

However, if you stepped through the data in time you would discover that something unexpected was happening over the Antarctic. Gradually over the course of a year, ozone concentrations began to decrease over the South Pole. As time progressed, this depletion became more and more pronounced. The media quickly picked up on the story and gave the phenomenon a name: the *ozone hole*. Something was reducing the concentrations of ozone over the Antarctic continent.

Ozone is an unstable molecule. Left to its own devices, the O_3 molecule will decay back to an oxygen molecule and an oxygen radical. This maintains an equilibrium in the upper atmosphere between ozone and oxygen molecules: The two molecules are constantly passing the extra oxygen atom back and forth in a never-ending game of molecular table tennis. Naturally, the rates of production and destruction of ozone are not always the same. Production and decay rates are dependent upon the intensity of ultraviolet (UV) radiation from the sun, the latitude of the location of the UV-bombarded oxygen molecule, the seasonal weather patterns, and so on. These variations, however, should be cyclic and the average yearly ozone concentration over a given latitude should remain relatively constant from year to year.

It has long been known that chlorofluorocarbons (more commonly called CFCs) react with ozone, causing it to form other chemical compounds. It was not until the reduction of atmospheric ozone was noticed that meteorologists, atmospheric scientists, and environmental scientists began to examine the total output of CFCs in industrialized countries. CFCs, as it turns out, are everywhere. Refrigeration and air conditioning units use CFCs (marketed under the name *Freon*) as coolant. Spray cans use CFCs to pressurize the contents (CFCs in spray cans were banned in the United States in 1978 for other reasons, but they are still widely used in other countries). CFCs are prevalent in the manufacture of foam plastics such as Styrofoam. CFCs are used as industrial solvents, and often wind up evaporated into the atmosphere or poured into landfills.

It seems a logical assumption that with all of the uses of CFCs around the world, large quantities are entering our atmosphere and destroying the ozone production and decay balance. Unfortunately, it is difficult to prove that CFCs are responsible for the ozone hole. In addition, there are some studies underway that may indicate that the drop in ozone over the Antarctic may be part of some natural, long-term cycle of ozone production and decay. As of the time of this writing, some evidence has come forth indicating that ozone production might be, once again, on the rise.

Humans have always been reactive rather than preventative. As a whole, we tend to respond to emergencies rather than defining a potential problem and taking steps to make sure the problem never arises. Often, dangerous street intersections are not given a traffic signal until an accident or a death has occurred at that corner. Likewise, financial and political concerns take precedence over certain environmental concerns. It seems likely that the amounts of greenhouse gases, CFCs, and chemical compounds that humans are pumping into the atmosphere are throwing off the equilibrium that the atmosphere has settled on as a natural balance. It also seems likely that once this equilibrium is out of balance, it will be difficult, if not impossible, to restore the situation to its former condition.

Earth's Protective Covering

If chemistry had never conspired to sheath the earth in a blanket of ozone, life as we know it may never have formed. Certain carbon chains essential to life cannot form in the presence of ultraviolet radiation, because the radiation breaks down the chemical bonds that hold these carbon chains together. Ozone is nearly opaque to ultraviolet radiation, scattering much (but not all) of the UV rays harmlessly into space. Now that life has a secure foothold, what would it mean if our ozone layer were suddenly removed? Ultraviolet radiation would destroy components of carbon-based life. Incidents of melanoma, cancer, and birth defects would increase dramatically.

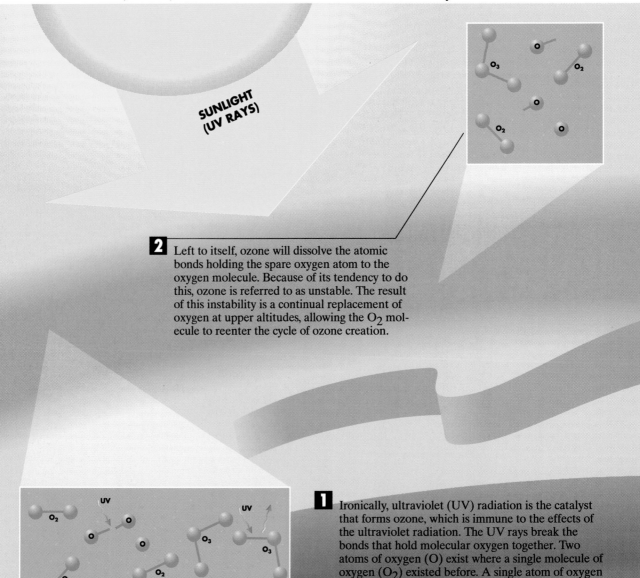

SUNLIGHT (UV RAYS)

2 Left to itself, ozone will dissolve the atomic bonds holding the spare oxygen atom to the oxygen molecule. Because of its tendency to do this, ozone is referred to as unstable. The result of this instability is a continual replacement of oxygen at upper altitudes, allowing the O_2 molecule to reenter the cycle of ozone creation.

1 Ironically, ultraviolet (UV) radiation is the catalyst that forms ozone, which is immune to the effects of the ultraviolet radiation. The UV rays break the bonds that hold molecular oxygen together. Two atoms of oxygen (O) exist where a single molecule of oxygen (O_2) existed before. A single atom of oxygen will bond with molecular oxygen, forming the triad O_3, or ozone. Ultraviolet radiation is reflected by molecules of ozone back into space, a process referred to as scattering.

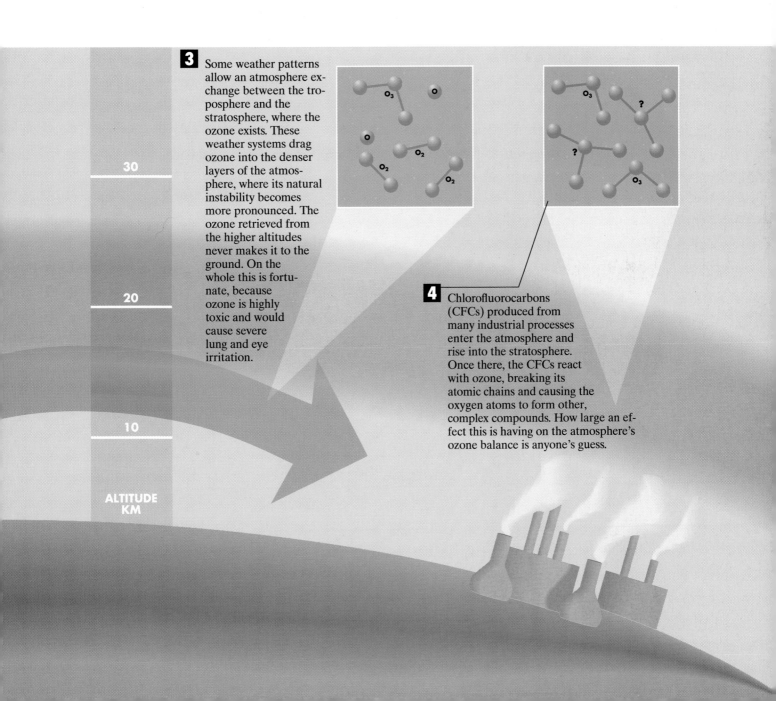

3 Some weather patterns allow an atmosphere exchange between the troposphere and the stratosphere, where the ozone exists. These weather systems drag ozone into the denser layers of the atmosphere, where its natural instability becomes more pronounced. The ozone retrieved from the higher altitudes never makes it to the ground. On the whole this is fortunate, because ozone is highly toxic and would cause severe lung and eye irritation.

4 Chlorofluorocarbons (CFCs) produced from many industrial processes enter the atmosphere and rise into the stratosphere. Once there, the CFCs react with ozone, breaking its atomic chains and causing the oxygen atoms to form other, complex compounds. How large an effect this is having on the atmosphere's ozone balance is anyone's guess.

30

20

10

ALTITUDE
KM

Nimbus 7's Coverage of the Earth

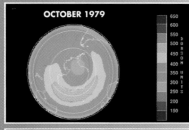

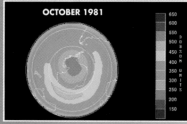

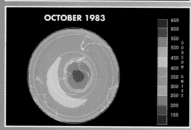

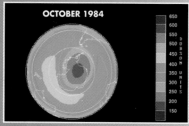

Nimbus 7, equipped with the *total ozone mapping spectrometer (TOMS)*, was placed into a south-to-north polar orbit in 1979.

The results These side panels (here and on the opposite page) graphically represent the data obtained from the TOMS instrument over a 12-year period from 1979 to 1990. The month of October was chosen because the Southern Hemisphere is just coming out of spring and entering summer during this period. It is during this time that ozone depletion is the most pronounced. The growth of the depletion zone over the Antarctic becomes quite noticeable as the years progress: Expected normal ozone levels for the region over the Antarctic are around 350 Dobson units, which places the ozone levels in the depletion zone at around 50% of normal levels by October 1990.

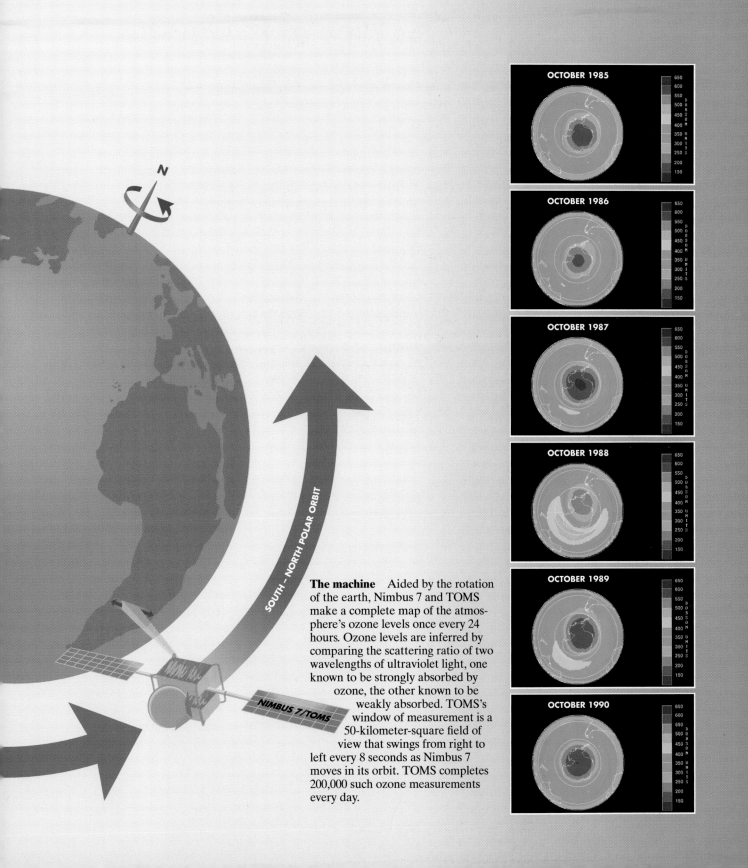

OCTOBER 1985

OCTOBER 1986

OCTOBER 1987

OCTOBER 1988

OCTOBER 1989

OCTOBER 1990

SOUTH - NORTH POLAR ORBIT

NIMBUS 7/TOMS

The machine Aided by the rotation of the earth, Nimbus 7 and TOMS make a complete map of the atmosphere's ozone levels once every 24 hours. Ozone levels are inferred by comparing the scattering ratio of two wavelengths of ultraviolet light, one known to be strongly absorbed by ozone, the other known to be weakly absorbed. TOMS's window of measurement is a 50-kilometer-square field of view that swings from right to left every 8 seconds as Nimbus 7 moves in its orbit. TOMS completes 200,000 such ozone measurements every day.

ETCETERA

CONTENTS

AROUND THE BEGINNING of the seventeenth century, Galileo Galilei created what was perhaps the first meteorologic device. Fascinated with vacuums, Galileo discovered that placing a long, vertical glass tube with a bulb at the top in a beaker of water caused the water to rise up the tube without the aid of a vacuum. The amount of water drawn into the tube from the beaker varied depending on the temperature of the air. If the air was cold, more water was drawn up as the air inside the tube contracted. Although it was crude and could not determine absolute temperatures, Galileo is commonly credited with having invented the first thermometer.

The reason the water was drawn into the tube without the aid of a vacuum mystified Galileo until his death, but one of his students, Evangelista Torricelli, correctly deduced that the water was being drawn into the tube from the beaker by the weight of the atmosphere pressing down on the surface of the water in the beaker. Torricelli decided it would be more practical to replace the water with a denser liquid: mercury. The higher density of the mercury meant that a smaller volume of liquid would be required for the same effect. By filling a 3-foot tube, open at only one end, with mercury, and then submerging the tube upside-down in a beaker, Torricelli observed that the column of mercury in the tube descended to a height of 30 inches, leaving a vacuum at the top of the tube. Galileo's early thermometer was the forerunner of Torricelli's barometer, a device used for measuring atmospheric presssure. The age of exact measurements of meteorologic phenomena had begun.

Things progressed rapidly from this point, and a host of other weather-recording devices were added to the meteorologist's arsenal over the centuries: *hygrometers* for measuring relative humidity, *anemometers* to measure wind speed and direction, and *rain* and *snow gauges* for measuring precipitation, to name a few. What could be considered the first weather map was drawn in 1820, and was based on information collected by mail from throughout Europe. Naturally, by the time the map was assembled, the weather system described by the map had already run its course. Considered an interesting academic exercise, the weather map was considered of little or no practical value until 1843, the year the telegraph was invented. Information from hundreds of ground stations could now be coordinated, and real benefit could be obtained from up-to-the-hour weather data.

The last 50 years have seen remarkable strides in weather data collection equipment. It was soon realized that the military radar device used to detect wartime aircraft could also be used to collect weather information. The need to minimize troop and ship

loss due to inclement weather during World War II resulted in the development of electronic computers that were applied to weather forecasting. In 1960, the United States
launched the first weather satellite, Tiros I, and plunged the world into an era of weather
detection and prediction that permanently changed humans' relationship with the
weather.

Prior to just three or four years ago, a book that explained weather phenomena
would conclude by instructing the home weather hobbyist on how to construct home-
made anemometers, rain gauges, and barometers. Perhaps some of the more
sophisticated hobbyists with access to amateur radio equipment could contact other hobbyists and share data collected by these home-built meteorologic devices. Now, thanks to
the infiltration of the home by personal computers and the establishment of nationwide
computer networks, the home hobbyist can tap into most of the same sources of weather
information that are used by professional meteorologists. For a relatively low cost, anyone interested in the weather can access the latest satellite image, obtain current ground
station readings from around the country, see current weather prediction models as forecast by the National Weather Service, and have on-line conferences with hundreds of
other people interested in weather analysis.

PART EIGHT

The Tools of the Modern Meteorologist

I N THE LATE 1970s and early 1980s, the United States began a very successful program of earth observation weather satellites called the Geostationary Operational Environment Satellite (GOES) program. The sophisticated satellites were placed into a *geosynchronous orbit*, an equatorial orbit designed to keep the satellite over a fixed position on the earth at an altitude of 22,240 miles. This orbital configuration allows the GOES program to continually monitor atmospheric activity over the entire continental United States, Mexico, and Canada. The GOES plan calls for two satellites to be in operation at any one time; *GOES-WEST* is the name of the position over the western coast of the United States, and *GOES-EAST* is the name of the position over the eastern United States.

From 1986 to 1994, a series of launching mishaps (including scheduling delays caused by the explosion of the space shuttle Challenger in January of 1986) and poor planning left the United States with a single weather satellite, GOES 7, in the western position. The United States relied on luck and borrowed equipment to keep its weather surveillance satellite system intact. For instance, in 1993 the United States borrowed an aging European satellite, Meteosat-3, to help maintain weather coverage.

The National Oceanic and Atmospheric Administration (NOAA) made good use of these years, however, and continued development on a new generation of GOES satellite systems. On April 14, 1994, one of these new-generation satellites, temporarily dubbed GOES-I, was successfully placed into a geosynchronous position next to the existing GOES 7. When the system was finished testing in mid-1994, the satellite was moved to its permanent eastern observation position and officially renamed GOES 8. (GOES 7 will continue operations until 1995, when it will be replaced by a sister satellite to GOES 8.)

Prior to GOES 8, weather satellite systems were only capable of providing imagery of their coverage area every 40 minutes. This slow response was due to the fact that the satellite had to spin rapidly about its axis in order to stabilize itself in orbit. This meant that the satellite could only image a portion of its coverage area during the brief interval that the camera lens was actually pointing at the earth; the rest of the time the satellite camera was pointing toward empty space.

Over the course of 40 minutes, a complete image of the coverage area would be assembled from the bits and pieces collected by the old GOES system. The newest generation of GOES satellites, however, have overcome this problem with improved technology for stabilizing the satellite's orbit: It no longer has to spin. This improvement alone allows the satellite to transmit complete images every 10 to 15 minutes.

The new satellites also have an improved version of a sensor called a sounder. The *sounder* allows the satellite to monitor atmospheric temperature and humidity by measuring the amount of infrared radiation that reaches the spacecraft. The sounder is capable of taking these measurements from different atmospheric altitudes, allowing the satellite to obtain a complete atmospheric temperature profile on demand.

By using the sounder, meteorologists will no longer have to rely on cloud patterns and motions to determine air movement. The sounder gives these researchers the ability to sample temperature profiles of clear air for clues as to the current dynamics in the atmosphere. In addition, the improved sounder can examine up to 19 different wavelengths of infrared radiation, allowing researchers to use this information to retrieve data on atmospheric concentrations of greenhouse gases such as carbon dioxide, water vapor, and methane.

Technological advances have breathed new life into a century-old technique for determining upper air movements. Balloons released into the atmosphere at regular intervals have been fitted with new, inexpensive electronics that return information collectively called soundings. Soundings should not be confused with the sounder sensor on the GOES systems, although they do have a common aim: Their purpose is to return temperature and dew-point temperature profiles of the upper atmosphere. Electronic devices called radiosonde on sounding balloons allow researchers on the ground to sample temperature and humidity as the balloon ascends. A modified radiosonde called a rawinsonde allows the device to be tracked by radar or other method for exact measurements of upper-level wind speeds.

One of the major advances to come out of the United States's war effort during World War II was the development of radar. *Radar*, which stands for *radio detection and ranging*, is a particle detection system; it emits a radio frequency pulse and listens for the echo of the pulse reflected off of a distant object. Although originally developed to detect movement of aircraft and naval ships, it was soon realized that radar could help detect and track storm activity by reflecting the emitted radio waves off of water drops, ice particles, and other particulate matter within a storm cell.

All electromagnetic radiation, such as visible light, radio waves, infrared radiation, and so on, is susceptible to an effect called Doppler shifting, or the Doppler Effect. The characteristic wavelength of an electromagnetic signal emitted by a moving object changes with respect to the receiver of those signals. The *frequency* of a signal is the measurement of the number of crests of the signal wave received in a given space of time. Therefore, the shorter the wavelength, the higher the frequency.

If an object emitting or reflecting an electromagnetic signal is approaching a receiver, the received wavelength is shorter than it was when it left the emitting object, which results in a higher frequency. If the emitting or reflecting object is moving away from the receiver, the wavelength is longer when it is received than when it was emitted, and the frequency is correspondingly lower. One common example of the Doppler effect can be experienced as a train approaches: The sound of the train's whistle becomes higher-pitched as it approaches the observer, then suddenly becomes lower in pitch after it passes the observer and recedes into the distance.

In the late 1960s, radars were coupled with computers to take advantage of the Doppler effect. The result was the *Doppler radar*, a modified radar whose return pulse contained more information than simple location and distance. By using computers to numerically compare the wavelength of the radar pulse when it left the radar with the same pulse as it returned, the Doppler radar is able to determine an object's location, distance, speed, and direction of travel with respect to the radar. In addition, by measuring the intensity of the returned signal, Doppler radars are able to determine the relative density of the objects under surveillance.

Instantly, a world of information became available to meteorologists. Now, not only can the position of a storm cell be detected, but information regarding a storm's direction of travel and speed can be obtained. As computers became more powerful as well as less expensive, sophisticated computer *algorithms*, or encoded sets of instructions, could use the radar data to infer more information about the storm. Examining the signal-strength data, these numerical algorithms can reveal the relative amount of precipitation inside the storm system. By looking very closely at the velocity information returned, rotational directions and velocities of mesocyclones, tornadoes, and hurricanes can be determined. By examining the history of storm positions, velocities, and strengths, and by numerically projecting these values into the future, accurate predictions of storm activity can be made.

The National Weather Service (NWS) has established an ever-growing network of Doppler radars across the United States. By coupling the information from these radars with the power of satellite monitoring, storm prediction, detection, and tracking has become extremely reliable in this country. Throughout the 1990s, the NWS will be deploying more advanced Doppler radar systems into this network. The improved capabilities and coverage areas of these systems will allow the NWS to give the population more lead time to prepare for approaching storms, tornadoes, and hurricanes.

Other modifications to the United States weather network are promised in the 1990s, the most radical of which is a system referred to as the Automatic Surface Observing System, or ASOS. ASOS is a suite of automated surface monitoring sensors designed primarily to fully automate weather observations. Using an advanced network of sensors to monitor land and ocean surface conditions such as temperature, humidity, pressure, wind speed and direction, cloud ceiling height, visibility, and precipitation, ASOS is intended to pass off weather information directly to the NWS and the National Oceanic and Atmospheric Administration (NOAA) without human intervention.

On March 31, 1994, Vice President Al Gore announced an initiative to further update the warning network. The NOAA maintains a system of 350 radio stations referred to as the NOAA Weather Radio, which reaches approximately 75% of the United States's population. Although the NOAA Weather Radio uses the nation's advanced network of Doppler radars, satellites, and other tools to provide a timely warning to local residences, 25% of the country is not covered, and in areas that do have access, the radio must be on in order for the weather warnings to be received.

Gore's initiative calls for the coverage area of the NOAA Weather Radio network to be expanded to include 95% of the United States. In addition, emergency warnings will be preceded by a special tone that will automatically turn on specially equipped radios to the Weather Radio network. Although this service is already currently available, the automatic radios are very expensive. Part of the Gore initiative will be to provide that same capability in low-cost ($25–$35) units available for home purchase.

Two Common Meteorological Tools: GOES and Doppler Radar

Two tools of the modern meteorologist are the orbiting Geostationary Operational Environment Satellites (GOES) and Doppler radar, which provide satellite imagery and sounder data.

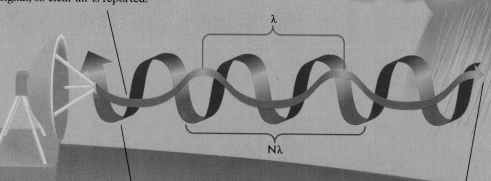

DIRECTION OF STORM MOTION

4 As the Doppler radar rotates its dish, it transmits a radio pulse at a known wavelength at each 1° position. The radar pauses listens until it hears a return signal or until enough time has passed to allow a signal to travel to the end of its range and return. In the latter case, the radar designers assume that there was nothing out there to reflect the signal, so clear air is reported.

λ

$N\lambda$

6 In this example, the storm system is moving directly toward the radar. Due to Doppler shifting, the wavelength of the returning signal is shorter than the wavelength of the original signal. When the signal returns, computers networked to the radar use the information obtained by calculating the difference between the two wavelengths as well as strength of return signal, to determine such factors as location, intensity, and motion of the storm system.

5 The radio pulse encounters particulate matter in a storm system: either water droplets, ice crystals, or dust and debris. Depending on the material, a certain percentage of the signal is reflected back toward the radar. The rest of the signal is either absorbed or scattered by the material.

1 Launched into an equatorial orbit and positioned at an altitude of 22,240 miles, two GOES satellites hover over their assigned fixed positions on the equator. The satellites' orbital velocity keeps pace with the axial spin of the earth, which allows the satellites to remain in a fixed position with relatively little energy.

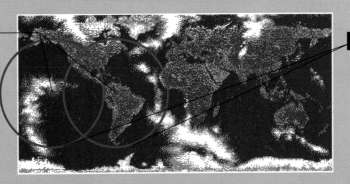

2 The combined coverage area of GOES-WEST and GOES-EAST includes all of South and Central America and most of North America. Currently, GOES-WEST is assigned to the satellite GOES 7, which is part of the pre-1990 generation of weather observation satellites. The GOES-EAST position has been unoccupied since GOES 6 reached the end of its five-year life span in 1989. The position was taken by GOES-8, part of a new generation of GOES satellites, in mid-1994.

3 This image was taken from GOES 7 on August 11, 1993 at 10:00 GMT (Greenwich mean time). All GOES imagery is transmitted to earth, or *downlinked*, as a gray-scale representation. The image is made up of 1,200 × 600 picture elements, or *pixels*, each of which represents a digital number from 0 to 63 representing the intensity of the energy being measured in that area. This image, for example, is a gray-scale representation of a GOES downlink with the pixel values representing energy values in the visible light range. Notice the horizontal line near the top and bottom of the image; this is due to data dropping out while the satellite was transmitting those rows of data.

7 As they can with the satellite image, computers can transform the digital data returned by the Doppler radar into visible images that human brains can more easily understand. This image and the one below represent two interpretations of the same storm. This image represents return signal strength reported as a unit of reflectivity called a dBZ. Reflection intensity increases as the numbers increase. The line of the storm front is clearly visible in the lower left corner of this reflectivity image.

8 This image is a measure of the velocity of the same storm system. Positive values indicate velocity away from the radar in meters per second, while negative values indicate velocity toward the radar in meters per second. See the small, red blobs imbedded in the approaching storm front? They have a strong velocity in the opposite direction of the rest of the storm. This may indicate a rotation inside of the storm system, possibly a mesocyclone.

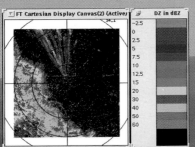

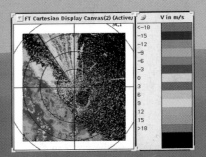

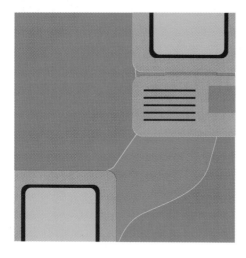

Weather in Cyberspace

N THE LATE 1970s and early 1980s, a collection of academic computer researchers began the construction of a wide-area computer network between university-based computers running an operating system called UNIX. The method of data transfer between any two machines was based on a *protocol*—a mutually agreed-upon standard for data transfer—called UUCP, or UNIX-to-UNIX CoPy. UUCP transfers information by picking up a phone and dialing a neighboring computer to deposit its message. If the receiving computer is not the message's end target, it calls another computer to pass along the information. It often took hours, or even days, for a piece of information to get where it was going.

While this UUCP user-based network, or *USENET*, was being developed, researchers at the Department of Defense began their own high-speed wide-area network. Dubbed *DARPANET*, the system relied not on phone lines, but on high-speed dedicated cross-country wires (sometimes leased from the phone company) to transmit its information. The data delivery was significantly faster, but the Department of Defense researchers also wanted access to university data and research systems. USENET and DARPANET were eventually bridged in a system referred to as *ARPANET*.

Over the next decade, various other information networks across the country with such esoteric names as BITNET, SPAN, and FidoNet would join the ever expanding ARPANET. Funding for much of the system was provided by a grant from the National Science Foundation (NSF), but the responsibility for control of this network of networks was relegated to no central authority: The system was self-regulating and continuing to grow. Eventually, the Department of Defense became concerned about security issues and dropped out of the system, and the network of networks adopted its now well-familiar name, the Internet. Internet gateways in other countries known as backbone sites paid for transatlantic and transpacific communications to the United States. The Internet has gone international.

Although the Internet grew, its core constituency was still academia, research labs, educational institutions, and nondefense-related government agencies throughout the world. The Internet represented a huge intellectual base that commercial organizations wanted to access. The

NFS and the business community worked out an agreement under which NFS funding of the Internet would be reduced to zero by the mid-1990s in return for commercial access to the network. Each site was now responsible for paying its own bills, but by this time the Internet was such a part of researchers', government officials', and business people's lives that no institution dropped out of the system. Paying for Internet access was now a normal cost of doing business.

In the first few years of the 1990s, it became obvious that companies could gain additional income by providing Internet access to home computer users. Fee-based dial-in services such as CompuServe, America Online, BIX, and GEnie began bridging the gap between home computer users and the Internet. Networks of dial-in *bulletin board systems* (*BBSs*), dial-in computers owned and operated by home computer hobbyists, also joined the fray. The home computer user was still at a disadvantage, however, as access to the Internet via these mechanisms was limited by the relatively low speeds of the home computer modem. Access via computer workstations at large universities, government agencies, and commercial organizations allowed much greater access rates than could be obtained by modems. A standard rate of transfer for home computers is 14,400 bits per second, while a typical college workstation has access to the Internet over special cable lines that allow access rates of over 1 million bits per second.

As of the time of this writing, home cable companies and telephone services are experimenting with ways of bypassing the modem and allowing computers direct high speed access into the Internet. On the East Coast, for instance, in some communities cable companies allow direct access to high speed connections over standard cable television wiring. In addition, libraries and other public institutions are installing Internet download workstations to allow people without computers access to the Internet.

As most of the Internet sites are still at academic and government institutions, there is a great deal of weather data and imagery available. Some of the fee-based access services allow for retrieval of some of this information via their own file transfer methods. In these cases, consult your fee-based service for the best way to download and use this data. Fee-based services often provide a less intimidating interface that makes finding and retrieving the information you want simpler. The disadvantage is that the user is usually presented with information after it has been "massaged" into shape by the fee-based service. Since these services have a limited amount of data storage capacity, they tend to pick and choose the weather information they offer carefully.

For unrestricted access to the data, along with the freedom to browse through vast amounts of historical information relating to weather data, it is necessary to go directly to the horse's mouth: the Internet itself. Weather data is available on the Internet in vast databases and archives stored on machines throughout the network. These archive computers allow users to access the information free of charge (minus connect time charges via the on-line service of choice), and the information is reliable and well maintained. Often, these weather database storage sites maintain information on interesting weather events such as Hurricane Andrew or the Blizzard of '93.

Internet commands for accessing this information are beyond the scope of this book, but there are many excellent references on the topic. In brief, there are currently two main methods for access: ftp, or file transfer protocol; or, if the user is fortunate enough to have direct access to a high-speed connection, access can be provided via the National Center for Supercomputing Applications (NCSA) multimedia interface to the Internet: Mosaic. *Ftp* is a get-your-hands-dirty method for remote logging into the weather archive computer and manually browsing through potentially hundreds of files. *Mosaic* allows a cleaner, more intuitive interface to the Internet, often allowing the user to view a small representation of the data before accessing it. The disadvantage of Mosaic is that it requires very high-speed connections to be useful, and the site containing the data must be registered in the Internet as a Mosaic site.

Regardless of the method the weather hobbyist uses (fee-based service, dial-in Internet access, or direct high speed connection) the Internet provides a wealth of information. Amateur weather watchers no longer content with home-built weather vanes, barometers, and other weather monitoring equipment can now play in the major leagues. Access to the Internet means access to the vast amounts of data available from institutions such as the National Weather Service; the NWS parent organization, the National Oceanic and Atmospheric Administration; university databases; and national weather forecasting centers. Up-to-the-minute GOES imagery can be *downloaded*, or transferred, directly to your home computer. Numerical models and forecast figures can be brought directly to your machine for easy access. The truly ambitious can do more than look at the images, numbers, and forecast models. Home weather watchers can write their own computer programs to manipulate this data and perform image processing on the satellite data.

Weather in Cyberspace: Gathering Weather Data over the Internet

There are literally thousands of Internet sites throughout the world that are depositories for weather images, data, and forecasting outputs—and this number increases daily. Here are just a few locations at which valuable information can be found. All depositories are given either as ftp site names and locations, or as Mosaic uniform resource locators (URLs). If you are unfamiliar with accessing Internet sites by either ftp or Mosaic, please consult a text on the topic, such as *How the Internet Works* (Ziff-Davis Press, 1994), or *How to Use the Internet* (Ziff-Davis Press, 1994).

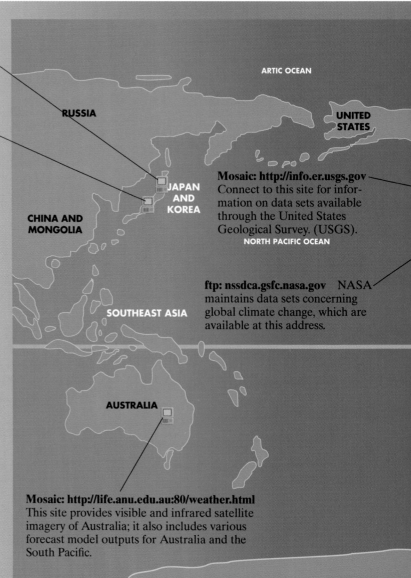

ftp: hydro.iis.u-tokyo.ac.jp data/noaa
From this site, you can get compressed images of Japan and the western Pacific region.

Mosaic: gopher://gopher.ncc.go.jp:70/11/INFO/weather
Files at this site include hourly Japanese weather conditions and forecasts in Japanese.

Mosaic: http://info.er.usgs.gov
Connect to this site for information on data sets available through the United States Geological Survey. (USGS).

ftp: nssdca.gsfc.nasa.gov NASA maintains data sets concerning global climate change, which are available at this address.

Mosaic: http://life.anu.edu.au:80/weather.html
This site provides visible and infrared satellite imagery of Australia; it also includes various forecast model outputs for Australia and the South Pacific.

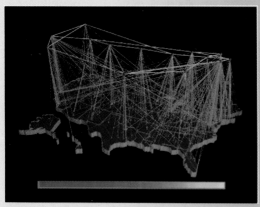

(Image courtesy of the National Center for Supercomputing Applications.)

The Internet is a vast network of networks under no central control. Although it has been around in one form or another for 15 years, it has recently gained the attention of the media and the public because of its vast resources and its availability. Although a few attempts have been made to map the Internet (one such attempt is pictured here), no one can completely succeed because of its growth rate. Some estimates show Internet sites to be growing at a rate 10% to 15% per month.

ftp: rainbow.physics.utoronto.ca pub/sat_images
This archive contains historical NOAA-11 and
NOAA-12 imagery of North America.

ftp: wmaps.aoc.nrao.edu pub/wx
Hourly GOES imagery of North
America is available at this address in both visible and infrared
wavelengths.

Mosaic: http://www.mit.edu:8001/weather
This archive includes hourly weather information and forecast updates for United
States cities. The home page provides a
point-and-click interface for accessing the
information.

ftp: cumulus.met.ed.ac.uk   This site
provides Meteosat images of the United
Kingdom made twice daily in both visible and infrared wavelengths.
Mosaic: http://web.nexor.co.uk   Here
you'll find Meteosat images of Europe
and Northern Africa in both visible and
infrared wavelengths.

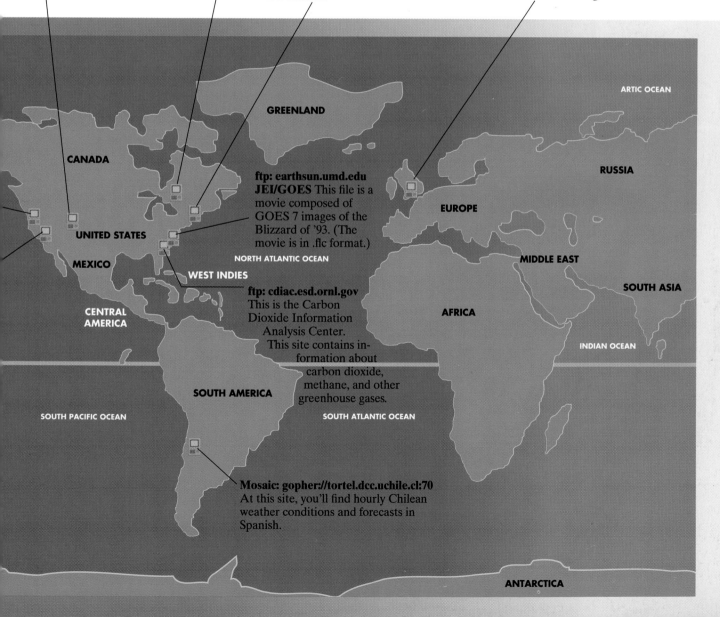

ftp: earthsun.umd.edu
JEI/GOES This file is a
movie composed of
GOES 7 images of the
Blizzard of '93. (The
movie is in .flc format.)

ftp: cdiac.esd.ornl.gov
This is the Carbon
Dioxide Information
Analysis Center.
This site contains in-
formation about
carbon dioxide,
methane, and other
greenhouse gases.

Mosaic: gopher://tortel.dcc.uchile.cl:70
At this site, you'll find hourly Chilean
weather conditions and forecasts in
Spanish.

ATTENTION TEACHERS AND TRAINERS
Now You Can Teach From These Books!

ZD Press now offers instructors and trainers
the materials they need to use these books in their classes.

- An Instructor's Manual features flexible lessons designed for use in a 10- or 15-week course (30-45 course hours).

- Student exercises and tests on floppy disk provide you with an easy way to tailor and/or duplicate tests as you need them.

- A Transparency Package contains all the graphics from the book, each on a single, full-color transparency.

- Spanish edition of *PC/Computing How Computers Work* will be available.

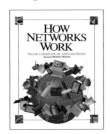

ZIFF-DAVIS ZD PRESS

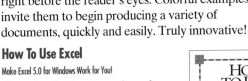
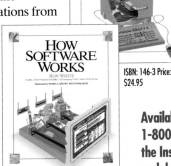

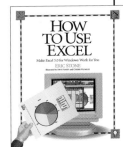
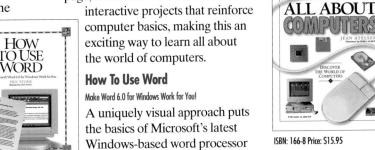

Ziff-Davis Press Survey of Readers

Please help us in our effort to produce the best books on personal computing.
For your assistance, we would be pleased to send you a FREE catalog
featuring the complete line of Ziff-Davis Press books.

1. How did you first learn about this book?

Recommended by a friend . . . . ☐ -1 (5)

Recommended by store personnel . . . . ☐ -2

Saw in Ziff-Davis Press catalog . . . .☐ -3

Received advertisement in the mail . . . . ☐ -4

Saw the book on bookshelf at store . . . . ☐ -5

Read book review in: _____ ☐ -6

Saw an advertisement in: _____ ☐ -7

Other (Please specify): _____ ☐ -8

2. Which THREE of the following factors most influenced your decision to purchase this book? (Please check up to THREE.)

Front or back cover information on book . . .☐ -1 (6)

Logo of magazine affiliated with book . . . . . .☐ -2

Special approach to the content . . . .☐ -3

Completeness of content . . . .☐ -4

Author's reputation. . . . .☐ -5

Publisher's reputation . . . .☐ -6

Book cover design or layout . . . .☐ -7

Index or table of contents of book . . . .☐ -8

Price of book . . . .☐ -9

Special effects, graphics, illustrations . . . . . .☐ -0

Other (Please specify): _____ ☐ -x

3. How many computer books have you purchased in the last six months? _____ (7-10)

4. On a scale of 1 to 5, where 5 is excellent, 4 is above average, 3 is average, 2 is below average, and 1 is poor, please rate each of the following aspects of this book below. (Please circle your answer.)

Depth/completeness of coverage	5	4	3	2	1	(11)
Organization of material	5	4	3	2	1	(12)
Ease of finding topic	5	4	3	2	1	(13)
Special features/time saving tips	5	4	3	2	1	(14)
Appropriate level of writing	5	4	3	2	1	(15)
Usefulness of table of contents	5	4	3	2	1	(16)
Usefulness of index	5	4	3	2	1	(17)
Usefulness of accompanying disk	5	4	3	2	1	(18)
Usefulness of illustrations/graphics	5	4	3	2	1	(19)
Cover design and attractiveness	5	4	3	2	1	(20)
Overall design and layout of book	5	4	3	2	1	(21)
Overall satisfaction with book	5	4	3	2	1	(22)

5. Which of the following computer publications do you read regularly; that is, 3 out of 4 issues?

Byte . . . . ☐ -1 (23)

Computer Shopper . . . . ☐ -2

Corporate Computing . . . . ☐ -3

Dr. Dobb's Journal . . . . ☐ -4

LAN Magazine . . . . ☐ -5

MacWEEK . . . . ☐ -6

MacUser . . . . ☐ -7

PC Computing . . . . ☐ -8

PC Magazine . . . . ☐ -9

PC WEEK . . . . ☐ -0

Windows Sources . . . . ☐ -x

Other (Please specify): _____ ☐ -y

Please turn page.

noted damase 12/14/09

PLEASE TAPE HERE ONLY—DO NOT STAPLE

6. What is your level of experience with personal computers? With the subject of this book?

	With PCs	With subject of book
Beginner................	☐ -1 (24)	☐ -1 (25)
Intermediate............	☐ -2	☐ -2
Advanced...............	☐ -3	☐ -3

7. Which of the following best describes your job title?

Officer (CEO/President/VP/owner)........ ☐ -1 (26)

Director/head.......................... ☐ -2

Manager/supervisor..................... ☐ -3

Administration/staff................... ☐ -4

Teacher/educator/trainer............... ☐ -5

Lawyer/doctor/medical professional....... ☐ -6

Engineer/technician.................... ☐ -7

Consultant............................ ☐ -8

Not employed/student/retired............ ☐ -9

Other (Please specify): _____ ☐ -0

8. What is your age?

Under 20............................. ☐ -1 (27)

21-29................................ ☐ -2

30-39................................ ☐ -3

40-49................................ ☐ -4

50-59................................ ☐ -5

60 or over........................... ☐ -6

9. Are you:

Male................................. ☐ -1 (28)

Female............................... ☐ -2

Thank you for your assistance with this important information! Please write your address below to receive our free catalog.

Name: _____

Address: _____

City/State/Zip: _____

Fold here to mail.

2281-13-16